D0065540

# HIGHER EDUCATION

*On Life, Landing a Job, and
Everything Else They Didn't Teach You
in College*

KENNETH JEDDING

RODALE

© 2010 by Kenneth Jedding

Rodale books may be purchased for business or promotional use or
for special sales. For information, please write to: Special Markets
Department, Rodale Inc., 733 Third Avenue, New York, NY 10017.

Printed in the United States of America
Rodale Inc. makes every effort to use acid-free ∞, recycled paper ©.

Book design by Christopher Rhoads

**Library of Congress Cataloging-in-Publication Data**

Jedding, Kenneth.
    Higher education : on life, employment, fulfillment, and everything else they
didn't teach you in college / Kenneth Jedding.
        p.     cm.
    Includes index.
    ISBN-13  978–1–60529–676–0 hbk.
    ISBN-10  1–60529–676–7 hbk.
    1. Young adults—Life skills guides.    2. College graduates—Life skills
guides.    3. College graduates—Employment.    4. College graduates—
Psychology.    I. Title.
HQ799.5.J42   2009
646.70084'2—dc22                                                                        2009051675

**Distributed to the trade by Macmillan**
2   4   6   8   10   9   7   5   3   1 hardcover

We inspire and enable people to improve their lives and the world around them

For more of our products visit **rodalestore.com** or call 800-848-4735

To Bette

# CONTENTS

# INTRODUCTION

YEARS AGO, WHEN I GRADUATED from college, I went into a local bookstore and asked the person behind the cash register where I could find *The Book*.

What I meant was the book that would tell me all the things I didn't learn in school: how to get a job, how to navigate friendship and love, how to maintain a good relationship with my family, and, above all, how to stay cool.

I wanted to know whether I'd majored in the wrong thing.

I wanted to know how to "get started," even if I didn't know what it was I wanted to do.

I wanted to know how to track down "my passion."

And how I should go about pursuing that passion once I knew what it was.

I wanted to know how to deal with relationships: new ones, old ones, breakups, and how to ready myself for "The One."

I wanted to know how to be with my parents.

And I wanted to know how to stay sane through the whole process.

In other words: I wanted to know *a lot*. And jumping into the great sea that is Life-after-College, with all its crosscurrents and crashing waves and changing tides, without *any* of this information, seemed a very dangerous leap. Which was why I went in search of a kind of life preserver: nothing epic, nothing too serious—just some guidance I could carry around with me, ideally in one hand.

Unfortunately, I was told no such book existed.

So I had to answer all those questions for myself.

☙

Needless to say, I wasn't equipped to write my own version of *The Book* for many years. But when I *had* done my best to answer all my own questions, I set about writing a version of what you hold in your hands: the book I believe every new college graduate should have the benefit of reading. It contains not just the wisdom I've gained over my own time spent in "the real world," but also the collective wisdom of many of my favorite people, friends and role models alike—all of whom have something to offer of enormous value to anyone just starting out—whether that's you, the graduate in your life, or indeed any curious reader in pursuit of a little advice.

So here you are: *Higher Education*. I hope it helps you—and those you share it with—achieve everything you desire . . .

And more.

# Part 1

# CAREERS

# CHAPTER 1

# YOU MAJORED IN THE RIGHT THING

*Map out your future, but do it in pencil.*

—JON BON JOVI

"I THINK I MAJORED IN *the wrong thing!*"

"*There aren't any jobs open for people with my major.*"

"*I majored in one subject, but now I want to do something else.*"

Does this sound like you?

Here's the thing: It sounds like a lot of people just out of college. But your major doesn't matter nearly as much as you probably think it does. It certainly doesn't matter as much to your prospective employers as it does to you. Of course, if you want to be a doctor but weren't premed, or if you want to be an engineer but never took an advanced math course, you'll have to go back and learn the fundamentals. But for most people, their college major is only the beginning of the story.

The *very* beginning. The "Once upon a time" part of your life.

Or at least it will be, soon enough. Trust me. What you majored in certainly says something about who you are and what interests you, but it isn't going to make or break your career. You're not stuck there.

The keys to your job prospects are your character, work ethic, and potential—in other words, your ability to give a prospective employer a reason to hire you. That's what employers are looking for, and that's what I'm going to talk about here.

I know what you may be thinking: *Yeah, right.*

Don't worry. We'll get there. We'll cover all the bases. For now, the important thing to digest is just this:

You majored in the right thing.

Really.

You did.

☙

Still need convincing?

Let's say you majored in French, but you don't want to be a language instructor, translator, professor, or interpreter at the United Nations. You've thought about it quite a bit, and what you really think you would enjoy is being an advertising copywriter. Not only that, but you've just come across an online job posting for an assistant copywriting position at an ad agency. But you researched it and found out they don't do ads in French. So now you're thinking, *Why would they hire someone who studied French?*

And while you're giving yourself a hard time for having wasted 4 years, the window of opportunity closes because the ad agency hires someone with a degree in . . . Spanish.

Why?

Because the Spanish studies grad showed up and made a successful case for herself.

And how did she do that?

Well, she said that even though she doesn't have any actual copywriting experience, she's eager to learn and willing to work hard.

So far, so good.

But what about the "Moment of Truth"?

What happened when the interviewer said, "But you majored in Spanish. This job is in copywriting. Our work's primarily in English."

What did she say?

"I majored in Spanish because I love Márquez and Allende, because I wanted to learn a new language, and because my favorite freshman seminar was 20th-Century South American Fiction and Political Change."

Wow!

Wait . . . what?

"Basically," she added, "I love words, I love language, and I love how people use language to persuade mass audiences."

And this, if you think about it, is *exactly* what an ad exec looking for an assistant copywriter wants to hear.

*But hold on!* you may be thinking now. *I don't speak a foreign language. I don't know anything about 20th-century South American fiction. Who is Márquez? Who is Allende? I didn't have a favorite freshman seminar. As a matter of fact, as a freshman I was just focused on having a good time, getting to class in one piece, and not embarrassing myself.*

It doesn't matter. The point is this: No matter how unrelated your major may seem to you, you should be proud of what you chose to study for 4 years, and you should find ways to make it relevant to *your story*.

Yes, even *your* major.

Keep reading.

⊙⊱

Part of the reason your major was "right" is that your choice of a major is an honest part of who you are, and that's exactly what a prospective employer wants to learn more about: *you*.

Virtually every person I've ever met in charge of entry-level hiring (and I have known many such people, across many different industries) insists that—assuming your résumé does not contain any blatant typos—the real deciding factors lie beyond the mere piece of paper.

They lie within you.

Think of it this way: A job interview is like a first date. Both you and your interviewer should be trying to figure out whether you want to spend a lot more time—probably all day, 5 days a week—in each other's company.

If you feel bad about your major, or you can't think of a single reason why it can be seen as relevant to the job—or if you've already decided that French is bound to be nothing more than a hobby down the road—you lose an opportunity to give the interviewer what he or she wants: some insight into how confident you are, what inspires you, and how you make decisions.

Here's the thing: People on first dates are interested in confident people.

People on first dates are interested in interesting people.

Your major tells a story about you—*if* you choose to tell it. So find a way to tell it!

Having majored in a discipline that reflects a passion, *whatever* that passion may be—film history or geography or playing the violin—is interesting, and that's a plus. Who wants to spend 40-plus hours a week with someone boring? *You* wouldn't.

Now maybe you're thinking, *But my major wasn't my passion. I'm not even sure I have a passion!*

That's okay, too. You just need to be a little more creative in telling your story. In the next chapter, I'll talk about how to take the first step—even if you don't know what you want to do. And later in the book, I'll have a lot to say about finding your passion. For now, just keep in mind that many hugely successful and thoroughly fulfilled people graduated with *absolutely no idea* of what they wanted to do or where to start. So don't worry.

Yes, even you, who majored in Gaelic translations of Renaissance literature.

∞

Let's consider a few more scenarios.

You majored in psychology, but you've since become really intrigued by the prospect of working for a film agency because you love movies. So you explore online and identify a few agencies. You send your résumé and a cover letter to, say, 10 of them.

Two weeks later, one of them invites you in for an interview. Congratulations!

Cut to:

INTERVIEWER: So why do you want to work for a film
   agency?

YOU: Well, I love movies.

INTERVIEWER: It says here you were a psychology
   major.

YOU: Yes, I chose psychology because I'm also really
   interested in what motivates people to make certain
   decisions and deal with crises—which, of course, is
   the arc for the plots of great movies. And psychology
   also taught me how to be convincing, which I think
   is a good foundation for being a successful negotia-
   tor.

Hired!

It isn't always so straightforward, of course—but you'd be
surprised by how often it is. Keep in mind that when an interviewer asks you about what you studied in college, she's not
really trying to brush up on whatever it is that you studied in
college. She's trying to learn about *you*—what you've accomplished, how you feel about it, and what makes you tick.

But maybe she's still not convinced. What if she frowns in
confusion at your résumé and throws you a fastball:

"So what makes you think you'd be a good [copywriter/film
agent]?" she asks, point-blank.

Moment of Truth Number Two.

If your major *really* doesn't seem to correspond with the
field you're trying to break into—if you're a biochem major sitting in that ad agency office, for example—well, naturally you'll
need to work a little bit harder to convince the senior copywriter
to hire you.

Put yourself in her position: Why should she take you over someone with a double major in communications and creative writing? What would convince *you* to give *you* a chance?

Don't worry. This question isn't as hard to answer as you may think it is.

In this instance, why not go to the interview armed with some examples of what you can do? Roll up your sleeves and take a stab at writing some ad copy for a product you know well, and then have a friend (preferably someone honest, or already in the field) look it over and give you feedback. Read up a little about how to write effective ad copy, or, if you have the time and money, take a 1-day course (see Chapter 3). The point is, if you can write good ad copy, or even copy that needs some polishing but shows promise, there's no reason why you shouldn't stand as good a chance as—if not better than—the woman who double-majored in communications and creative writing but showed up to her interview empty-handed.

Let's look at another example.

Say you majored in physical therapy. You always thought you'd become a therapist eventually, but now you're not quite ready to continue with the necessary training. Meanwhile, you've noticed that the YMCA where you've been taking dance classes has an entry-level job opening—in the Fund-Raising and Development Office.

And suddenly you think, *Hey.* That *might be interesting.*

So you send in your résumé, and, miracle of miracles, you're granted an interview. It's the night before, and you're trying to come up with a reason why the head of the Fund-Raising and Development Office should hire *you,* of all people.

Rehearse in advance, in your room, with an imaginary interviewer.

Picture your interviewer. She looks at your résumé and cuts right to the chase:

"What makes you qualified for this job?"

You say: "Well, I love to dance, which is why I started taking classes here—and I've been very impressed. The classes are fantastic. I think the Y is a great resource that too few people know about, and I really want to help it thrive. And because I majored in physical therapy—which I initially chose because I'm athletic and enjoy helping people—I've learned a lot of strategies for dealing with people's physical and psychological needs, and also about the importance of staying healthy. So I think all of these things would help me present the Y in a very favorable light to potential donors."

Great!

But will the director be convinced?

Maybe we need to take it a step further. How does physical therapy relate specifically to fund-raising and development?

Ask yourself, *Have I ever done anything remotely like fundraising?*

Okay. Let's brainstorm.

Remember that time you participated in a _____that led to _____?

There's a template. Can you fill in the blanks?

"Yes," you say, "I remember the time I participated in a *tailgate party* that led to my *arrest.*"

No!

(This is why we rehearse.)

Let's try again.

Was there a charity drive you led in college that helped to raise money?

Yes? Excellent!

Mention it at the interview. Now, *that's* impressive!

Ah . . . but the drive wasn't successful?

Then how about this:

Remember that charity drive you led in college that *didn't* raise much money, but you learned so much doing it?

That's it. That's just what the Fund-Raising and Development director wants to hear!

What? There was no charity drive, you say?

Well, then, here's a situation where your golden ticket might require a little advance legwork. Get on Google, or go to the library or a bookstore, and read up on how to be a successful fund-raiser. Maybe even make a list of all the companies you can think of that might be willing to donate to the Y.

*Your* Y.

The one you've come to love and want to help raise money for, so it can afford new facilities, state-of-the-art equipment, top-notch instructors, a smoothie bar, and a sauna.

Soon you'll be ready to nail the interview and get the job.

*But it doesn't matter whether I think I majored in the right thing or the wrong thing,* some of you are thinking now, *because I can't even get an interview!*

Well, you're not alone. The good news is that there are many ways to expand your network and get your foot in the door. It will probably even be through someone you already know (More on this in Chapter 3.)

But for now, telling yourself, "I majored in the wrong thing" is self-destructive. In every situation, we can choose either to

## SOME FAMOUS PEOPLE AND THEIR COLLEGE MAJORS

Bruce Bodaken, chairman, president, and CEO of Blue Shield of California: Philosophy

Kevin Costner, actor: Business marketing and finance

Katie Couric, broadcast journalist: American studies

Mario Cuomo, former governor of New York: English

Carly Fiorina, president, CEO, and chairman of the board of Hewlett-Packard: Medieval history and philosophy

Art Garfunkel, musician: Mathematics

Mia Hamm, soccer player: Political science

Mick Jagger, rock star: Economics

John F. Kennedy, president: History

Bruce Lee, martial artist/actor: Philosophy

Janet Reno, US attorney general: Chemistry

Sally Ride, astronaut: English

Willard Scott, broadcast weatherman: Religious studies

David Souter, Supreme Court justice: Philosophy

Steven Spielberg, director: English

Juanita Kidd Stout, federal judge: Music

tear ourselves down or to build ourselves up. The goal always, but especially now, at this really challenging time of your life, is to build yourself up.

So remember: You majored in *something*. And that something is a story about who you are and what you've learned and what you've gained. People want to hear that story. So when you do get your interview—and you will—dress appropriately, tuck in your shirt, comb your hair, and walk into that room confident that the person across the desk won't be thinking about your major so much as focusing on who *you* are and what you can bring to the table.

Bring it all.

CHAPTER 2

YOU DON'T NEED TO
KNOW WHAT YOU'RE
GOING TO DO . . .

*Wisdom consists not so much in knowing what to do, but
knowing what to do next.*

—HERBERT HOOVER

BUT YOU DO NEED TO start doing it. Now that you know it's
possible to move forward whatever your major happened to be,
new questions arise:

*"How do I take the first step?"*

*"Where do I start?"*

*"What if it's the wrong first step?"*

Every year I travel the country speaking to groups of college
seniors and new grads. As they enter the room, their faces tell
the whole story:

He-e-e-l-l-l-p-p-p!

They arrive visibly distressed—eyes wide, lips drawn—and
they usually fall into one of two categories.

1. Those who have no idea whatsoever of what they
want to do.

2. Those who *do* have an idea but aren't sure it's
   "right."

Does this sound familiar?

Then I talk for about 45 minutes, and, in 99 cases out of 100, the audience members are transformed into calm and inspired—and sometimes even exuberant—people.

I'm not a magician, so what's my secret?

In the course of those 45 minutes, I cover many areas, but I actually talk about one thing more than any other. I tell them that they need to get started *even if they don't know exactly what it is they want to do*. Of course, this also applies to those who *do* have an idea of what career they plan to pursue, because they're often beset by similar worries. Few people are 100 percent sure.

*"But what does 'Just get started?' mean?"* I hear a voice asking. *"How am I supposed to start doing 'it' if I don't know what 'it' is?"*

Or:

*"I have a pretty definite idea of what I want to do, but I'm afraid I'll be stuck in that field for the rest of my life!"*

Here's the secret. This is why you can truly relax:

## All roads lead to Rome.

I can almost hear your reply.

*"What the @#$%! does that mean?"*

A little story: Fifty years ago, long before our time, people used to say, "What the Sam Hill does that mean?" Because this millionaire, Sam Hill, built a museum in the middle of nowhere, in rural Washington, and no one could figure out why he put it there.

Feel better?

No?

Okay. Back to Rome. What I mean when I say all roads lead there is this:

## Skill sets are transferable.

And what does *that* mean? Now a story will definitely help.

I know a woman who graduated from college with a bachelor's degree in theater arts. She wanted to direct plays, and within 5 years, she was doing it. She became a successful theater director. And then she got tired of directing and decided that what she really wanted to be was a lawyer.

Imagine! What if you graduated with a degree in theater arts and then decided you wanted to be a lawyer? How would *that* feel? Or imagine becoming successful at the one thing you'd dreamed of doing all your life, and then realizing you actually wanted to do something else and had to start all over again from the beginning.

Yet it's not as strange as it seems. The woman became a successful lawyer.

Maybe your first reaction is *"Yeah, but what a waste of time her first career was."* That's how I would have reacted years ago. It would have seemed to me that someone should have told her, the day she graduated from college, "Forget theater. You should be a lawyer."

But skill sets are transferable, which means directing wasn't a waste of her time at all.

Think about it this way: What skills are common to these two fields?

To begin with, as a director, my friend was coaching actors to deliver convincing performances to an audience. Naturally. And as a lawyer? She became a litigator—the person who stands in front of a jury and makes a compelling case for her clients.

You see? My friend's directing experience was, in many ways, the *perfect* training for giving moving "performances" to juries. So her first career was hardly a waste of time. It was preparation.

But here's the key: When my friend "just got started" in her first career as a theater director, she wasn't thinking, *But this is just temporary. One day I'll be a lawyer.*

She didn't know.

She had no idea.

She was just doing the first thing with integrity, which means she did this as well as she could. She showed up on time, took the job seriously, and tried every day to be the best theater director she could be. Does that mean she was perfect? No. That she never had second thoughts? No. That she was always motivated? No. That she always enjoyed it? No.

But she'd decided to start there, and she did her best. *And that's all you need to do, as well.*

You don't have to know your path in advance. In fact, you usually can't.

To take this a step further: If you start in an area and you're not sure if it's right for you, it can still lead to an area that will be. So you can take a leap.

Getting back to my friend's case, there are other skill sets her two fields share: Both directors and lawyers need to have research skills and the ability to multitask.

The point is, as different as they may seem on a résumé, one feeds into the other.

So you can get started. Doing something.

Yes, even *that* thing, the one you're not so sure of.

Don't worry so much about where it will lead. That will become apparent later.

⊙⅋

Career experts say that, on average, people have three or even four careers.

Not jobs: *careers!*

I know, it's an exhausting idea. If someone had dropped that little pearl into my lap when I was 22 or even 25, I would have embarrassed myself by yelling: "I'm just trying to figure out how to be successful in *one* career, and you're telling me I need to pull off *four*?"

And how much time would I waste? Four careers? Wouldn't that take 20 years? Or 30?

But if someone had taken the time to explain to me that all roads lead to Rome—meaning that skills sets are transferable—I think I could have calmed down, because that changes the entire equation.

It means that, provided you always do the best job you possibly can, your time is *never* wasted—even if you don't love what you're doing, and even if you don't know what's going to come next. All you need to do right now is run with the leading career choice—or the best job prospect that's been offered to you, or maybe even the *only* job that's been offered to you—and take your first step.

And remember, most important: Your initial job—your initial *career*—is only your first stop, not your last.


## SIX DEGREES

Have you ever heard of *Six Degrees of Separation*?

It was a play, and then a movie with Will Smith, based on the idea that everyone on the planet is connected by no more than six degrees. You know someone who knows someone, who knows someone, who knows someone, who knows someone, who knows any sports star. Any movie star. A peasant girl halfway around the world. A president.

I love the Web site www.oracleofbacon.org. You can enter any actor and it links that actor to Kevin Bacon in very few steps, presumably six degrees or less. The idea is that Kevin Bacon has done so many movies, he's crossed everyone's path!


### Josh Hartnett

was in *The Black Dahlia* with Steve Eastin,

who was in *Rails and Ties* with Kevin Bacon.

Two degrees of separation.


### Katie Holmes

was in *Wonder Boys* with James Kisicki,

who was in *Telling Lies in America* with Kevin Bacon.

Again, two degrees of separation.

I wanted to find an example with six juicy degrees, so I put in Clark Gable. After all, the guy died in 1960! But I still found this:

## CLARK GABLE

was in *The Misfits* with Eli Wallach,

who was in *Mystic River* with Kevin Bacon.

Two degrees.

Incredible.

Now, here's the thing: The Six Degrees trick also works in Six Degrees of Professions.

So, let's say you're frustrated about where to begin. You don't know what you want to do.

You'll probably tend to think in terms of "career areas," which can be intimidating. There's:

Academia

The Arts

Finance

Health Care

Law

Media

Public Relations

Science

And that's to name just a few. Even if you *do* have an idea of what you want to do, these areas might seem like fortresses or prisons: hard to break into, and maybe even harder to get out of.

But they aren't.

So how can you hop from one to another?

More to the point, *can* you just hop from one to another?

Again, I'd ask you to forget the "areas," which are just labels, really, and think in terms of skill sets instead.

Another story:

I know a guy who was driving to the train station in a wealthy suburb of New York City when he saw a woman walking six dogs. He stopped the car and stared at her. His job in real estate was lucrative and prestigious, but he was bored . . . and he loved dogs. He knew he couldn't throw it all away to become a dog walker, but still, he felt frustrated by where *he* was in life, and intrigued by where this woman was.

I asked him and I'll ask you: How many degrees of separation do you think there are between real estate and professional pet care?

This is what we came up with: two.

Because of kennels.

Think about it. What are kennels, really? Little hotels for dogs and cats. They check in. They check out.

So how would my friend's work in real estate have prepared him for professional pet care?

Well, his career in real estate had taught him the business end: finding the right location, renting at the right price, administrating income and expenses for a rental property (specifically a hotel), and financing the project.

All he needed to do was learn more about the daily care of dogs and cats. He and his wife used to take care of his friends' dogs when they went on vacation, so he wasn't exactly starting from scratch there, either.

So back to the question: How many degrees of separation

are there? If you put real estate on one end, kennels in the middle, and pet care on the other end:

## Real Estate → Kennels → Pet Care

Two degrees.

It's true.

Everything is connected, and sometimes a lot more closely than we may imagine.

In fact, the first chapter of this book could have been called "Six Degrees of College Majors."

Just think back to that list of prominent, accomplished people on page 12. It is evidence that music majors can become groundbreaking federal judges, and math and engineering majors can become famous musicians or actors.

This is possible because you can apply whatever you've learned to new situations.

And yet . . . I know. You don't want to take a wrong step. When it comes to your career, whatever that may be, you want to make the *perfect* choice.


## FLASHBACK

To graduation day. Think of it: There you were, smiling for the camera, arms around your family and friends, looking fabulous in a cap and gown. (Love your hair!)

For some of you, the prevailing attitude was "Man, I'm glad *that's* over!" For others, it was "Wait a minute. Is the party really over? Do I *have* to leave?"

But I suspect that while you were standing there, you had

certain basic assumptions about what would follow. You probably figured:

- I have my whole life ahead of me!
- There will be plenty of fun days and nights.
- I'll have years with my old friends and the news ones I'll
  make.
- Maybe, at some point, I'll even get together with some-
  one special.

In other words, you took it for granted that life wasn't fro-
zen in time. You knew life would unfold. You *didn't* know the
how, what, where, or when of your future, but that was okay
with you.

Why, then, while smiling for the camera on graduation day,
are so many of us plagued by the idea that our *career* life is
stuck in that moment? As in, "Right now, standing here with my
arms around my friends and family and holding my mouth in a
good smile, I'm supposed to know *exactly* what I'm going to do
in my career: what field I'll go into, who's going to hire me (and
when), where it's going to lead, and how it will turn out."

How exhausting.

And yet, after the click of the camera and a slight pause, you
were able to put your arms down, step away from the pose, and
continue rolling with the ongoing "movie" of your life.

Here's the thing:

It's okay to approach your career the same way.

In fact, it's better than okay. It's natural. It's just a question
of trusting the process.

As Steve Jobs said, "You can't connect the dots looking forward; you can only connect them looking backward. So you have to trust that the dots will somehow connect in your future."

❧

So now you understand how all careers are connected by skill sets, such as with the woman who went from theater directing to law. The point here is: Take a step. You can only start from where you are. It doesn't have to seem exactly right. It doesn't have to be "perfect." You can adjust your direction along the way, and even have fun doing it. But first you have to start moving, say, to put a toe in the water.

*"Okay. I'm ready. I want to start moving. In fact, I'm more than ready. I'm dying to put my toe in the water. There's just one thing . . . where is the water?"*

Ah. Good question.

Keep reading.

# CHAPTER 3

# PUTTING YOURSELF OUT THERE

Action is the antidote to despair.

—JOAN BAEZ

SO YOU'RE JUST OUT OF school, and someone has already hired you! You had a job to report to the Monday after graduation!

I bow to you.

I salute you.

I high-five you.

You should still read this chapter, because either (1) you're lying, or (2) you're telling the truth, but you still need to know this: Very few things in life proceed so straightforwardly. So it's good to be prepared.

Here is the number one misconception among people who just graduated from college: They think something's seriously wrong with them if they don't just fall right into a job.

And here's the truth: For the majority of new grads, it will take a little while. And there is nothing seriously wrong with them.

So what happens in the meantime?

Well, if you were counting on a job to make you feel like a member of the "real" world—if you were convinced that having a job would bestow upon you "independence" and "financial freedom"—then if you don't get one right away, you'll probably feel like a failure. And you'll start to drive yourself crazy.

This is even more true if you're wallowing in debt (student and otherwise).

But you shouldn't feel like a failure.

Why? Because you aren't one.

*"But I am! I need a job!"*

Okay. *I'll* give you a job.

In fact, I'll give you two.


# JOB #1

*Keep yourself in a positive state of mind—in good physical and mental shape.*

This will make you more employable, not to mention happier throughout this challenging time. I'll talk more about staying in mental and physical shape later, in the chapters on Perspective, but for now, trust me: It's important. Just as important as what's on your résumé.


# JOB #2

*Put yourself out there.*

This is big.

What does it mean?

Let's look back for a minute.

The way it worked from grades K through 12 and then in

college was this: You did the work, and then your teacher told you how you did by giving you a grade.

So what happens after school? We think, *I'll get the job, and the boss will tell me how I did with regular feedback and maybe even the occasional raise.*

But if we don't get the job, or if we do and we're not happy in it, what then?

Job #2 is to become proactive.

What does that mean?

While it's good that you're looking for jobs, writing cover letters, sending out résumés, and hoping for interviews, it's not enough. Waiting for a reply is agonizing. And the truth is, your prospective employer probably has dozens of résumés and just one slot to fill, so you may not get one. A reply, that is. (Of course you'll get a job . . . eventually.)

So there's another angle to work, too. Instead of waiting for someone to hire you, you've got to take the first few steps. By which I mean attending talks and readings, visiting the career center, networking, and asking for informational interviews.

In other words: making things happen.

It's tricky, I know.

If you're frustrated that things aren't proceeding "on schedule"—whether you haven't figured out which career path to pursue, or you have, but you haven't been offered "the job" yet—it's easy to go on strike. Especially when going to a lecture sounds like a waste of time.

Think of it this way. You're reading this book. How's it making you feel? Better?

I give lectures and take questions afterward. I can see in people's faces that by the end of the talk, their trauma has often turned to relief, and many are smiling. People tell me that when they leave, they feel less afraid and more equipped to get started.

Here's the thing: Feeling better about your situation rather than paralyzed or depressed puts you a step closer to landing the actual job. So doing something like going to a career talk is just as effective as sending out your résumé. In the same way, reading this book—even if you're reading it at home—is a form of "putting yourself out there."

That *is* your power.

That *is* forward movement.

It's bringing you closer to figuring things out. The trick is to keep it going.

⊘ð

But I hear the voices again:

*"Why would I go to the career center? I hate that place."*

*"I'll go to the career center if you can promise me that, after an hour, they'll find me a job."*

Let's face it: Spending an hour in a career center probably won't get you a job. But it will get you closer to one.

You'll make new contacts, or something there will plant a seed that may sprout, say, 6 months down the road, leading you in an entirely new direction.

And more voices!

*"How will getting out there solve my problems? And besides, I'm broke."*

I get it.

It's no fun being broke, confused, and dependent. So it's

easy to think, *If the world delivers the job, I'll sign on. I'll take it. I promise.*

But I've found that the world doesn't work that way. Before "the world" hires you, "the world" wants to know what *you* are going to do for *it.*

You: "I'll show up when you give me a reason to."

THE WORLD: "No. You show up first. *Then* I'll give you the reason."

Ouch.

But once you get the hang of it, it's easy.

Let's say, for example, that you're interested in archaeology. And let's also say, for the sake of argument, that a local bookstore is hosting a reading by a woman who just wrote a book about archaeological digs.

You might be thinking, *Why should I go? No one's going to hire me there.*

But I'd ask you to close the laptop, put the phone away, and *go!*

Listen to her speak. Learn more about the field that interests you. Introduce yourself to the author when it's over. Without being too pushy, tell her what you liked about what she said.

And don't forget to pay attention to the people around you; they're there precisely because they have interests in common with you. Did anyone in the audience ask a question that revealed some expertise in the field? Why not introduce yourself to that guy when it's over, too? Yes, it's a little awkward, but force yourself. It will be easier next time.

Say, "Hi, I'm John, and I really liked what you said about

the Temple of Dendur. In fact, I'm exploring the possibility of working in archaeology or some related field for a year or so before applying to grad school."

If he has an opinion about this strategy or knows of an actual opportunity, maybe he'll mention it. And maybe he won't. So long as you're polite and respectful and you present yourself well, you have nothing to lose.

Then you'll go home, take a deep breath, pat yourself on the back (if you can reach back that far), and consider that what you did was big.

It might not feel so big.

It might feel like *I wasted my time, and for what? To introduce myself to someone who didn't really care. And by the way, I still don't have a job.*

But all you need to do is become a little bit better at taking these small steps, at finding the value in being a part of things, and something *will* happen.

In fact, that's exactly how things happen.

## NETWORKING

When I was younger, I could never understand the concept of networking. Did it involve standing around in a room full of people wearing name tags?

Who had the time?

And when I graduated from college, all I was thinking was that I needed a job. Now. "Acquiring contacts," which sounded like it would take forever, made no sense at all.

But what if I told you that *60 percent of jobs aren't advertised*? They come by word of mouth. They're filled through recommendations. Recommendations made by people who know people, or who recently met people who seem right for the job.

Which means you need to go on a Six Degrees treasure hunt: to meet someone who knows someone, who knows someone, who knows someone, who knows someone who will give you the job. The Kevin Bacon of your field.

It sounds like an impossible task, but it's not.

And sometimes it doesn't even take so many people.

More voices!

*"But wait a minute. If I network and meet someone, and it doesn't lead to anything real, no job, nothing, and all I have is this business card in my wallet—do you really expect me to spend another evening in the local hotel function room, drinking watered-down gin and tonics with a fake smile plastered on my face?"*

Enter Bob Dylan.

My favorite Dylan line is from the song "It's All Right Ma (I'm Only Bleeding)." The line is: "Say okay, I have had enough, What else can you show me?"

To me, it describes the way life is.

Think of it. Imagine feeling tired of working too hard, or tired of living in debt, or tired of not having a job, or tired of worrying, or tired of living at home, and you say, "All right! I've had enough!" As in: *Leave me alone! I'm done! I can't take it anymore!*

But life doesn't end there. So you have to add:

What else can you show me?

As in: I've had enough . . . but now I have to do a little bit more.

Gulp. Sound crazy?

But think of someone who gets her heart broken. That can lead to an "All right, I've had enough" moment, as in: *I'm bitter. I'm never going to get together with anyone else again. I give up.*

I once had my heart broken. A friend of my grandmother's said, at the time, "One door closes, another opens."

I swear, I wanted to slap her—and I would have, were I the slapping-little-old-ladies type. But I eventually came around to being able to ask the world, "Okay. What else can you show me?"

In other words: Okay. I have to try again.

Let's say your girlfriend says, "You don't listen to me," and eventually, frustrated, she dumps you. Or she says, "You don't spend enough time with me." So you learn to listen to the next one. Or spend more time with her. And as a result, the next relationship works. So you don't need to ask, "Why did I waste time with that first person?" Because the truth is, the first relationship was a step in the process. It actually prepared you for what would come next. Nothing is wasted.

I know that in my case, my wife, who came along years later, is a far better match for me than I ever could have realized before I learned the lessons of my big breakup.

So now let's think of this in relation to careers.

It's inevitable that you'll be up against job-related "heartache" at some point. Maybe your first job or career backfired, and now you have to reevaluate. Or you're stuck living at home for weeks or months or even longer, still feeling like you're at square one because you haven't gotten any job offer at all.

The thing to realize is this: This isn't just common, it's an essential part of the process. The question isn't "How did I end up back here, starting from scratch?" or even "What's wrong with me?" because I guarantee you, there are plenty of other gifted people in the same boat. And even those who *do* have jobs may see it the same way. The job doesn't always feel as great as they thought it would, so they, too, are thinking, *I've had enough!*

But you're not starting from scratch. By virtue of your experience, you're coming at things from a more informed position of strength.

The only real question you need to ask yourself is this: "Okay, so given that this is pretty standard stuff, what should I do next?"

In other words: What else can you show me?

So, when I talk about networking, let's not worry too much about name tags and lukewarm drinks in plastic cups. I'm talking about so much more.

Such as?

*Every single person you meet is part of your network.*

It's true. Networking isn't only about business cards and cocktail functions and "Hello my name is ____" stickers. Here are some examples of people who may not have a job to offer, or even valuable advice to share, but who may know someone who *does,* which is just as good.

Alumni

Classmates

Professors

Family

Friends' parents

Parents' friends

Neighbors

Past employers

Personal trainers, tennis/swimming coaches, yoga teachers, etc.

People you babysat for or mowed lawns for

Indeed, anyone you meet and reach out to with the words "I'm looking for a job, ideally one in _____, but I'm open to different possibilities" has the potential to help you out.

It's in people's nature. Most people *love* to establish connections and help people out in the process.

Now. Keep in mind that your tennis coach may not know anyone who needs an aspiring Web site designer *right now* (i.e., while you're practicing your serve). But you never know who his next tennis partner might be—and wouldn't it be a shame if it were a woman who owns her own consulting business and whose chief Web site designer needs an assistant pronto . . . and you didn't mention to your coach that *you're* looking for a job?

Maybe your tennis coach doesn't have any good connections at the moment. Maybe the couple you occasionally babysit for doesn't, either. So how do you build your network beyond the people you already regularly encounter?

Lectures, meetings, readings, reunions, parties, panel discussions, events based on invitations that, yes, you accept. How about that exhibit of paintings by the guy who was in Psych 101 with you 3 years ago? Anything that interests you is going to expose you to people who share your interests. You'll always leave with something.

This is the art of making things happen.

The art of learning how to present yourself, which is an ongoing process.

Of convincing yourself that your small efforts are actually

huge, and that the energy you invest in putting yourself out there will eventually be paid back to you in real results.

The art of being proactive and in the right place at the right time.

And ultimately, the art of gathering momentum and becoming a magnet, poised to attract a real opportunity.

CHAPTER 4

———— 〰️ ————

# MENTORS AND INTERVIEWS

Tell me about yourself—your struggles,
your dreams, your telephone number.

—PETER ARNO

## MENTORS

So. Let's say you just graduated and you want to work in public relations. You might start looking for a job by Googling local firms and sending out your résumé, but then time goes by and no one calls you for an interview.

(If it's *really* driving you crazy, skip ahead to page 230 in Part 4, Perspective, for a reality check. And come back when you're breathing easy again and are ready to proceed.)

So, what else can you do while you're waiting to hear back from prospective employers?

Well, as we've already discussed, you have to put yourself out there. One good way to do that is to explore your network for mentors.

Mentors are very good things. They can help you clarify why you want to go into a field—or, just as valuable, why

you don't. They can give you a realistic sense of what to expect and how to navigate problems as they arise. Sometimes
they can even lead to a job. People enjoy mentoring other
people. You just need to find the right mentor, or even more
than one.

Say your friend John's mom works in PR. Great! Your next
step is to ask to speak with her over the phone or, better yet,
meet with her in person, either at her office or at her house,
whichever she prefers.

At the meeting, ask her whatever you need to know, but be
focused, organized, and respectful. You can't just plop yourself
down on the sofa and say, "Can you give me a job?" or even
"Do you know anyone who'd give me a job?"

Why? Because if she thinks well of you and she knows of a
person or job, she'll suggest it herself. If you suggest it first,
you'll be putting her in an awkward position.

The main thing to remember is that this is an informational
interview for *both* people involved. You're interviewing her for
information, but she's also interviewing you to get a sense of
whether you're ready and right for the field. And you wouldn't
go into a "real" interview and say, "Can I have this job?"—
would you?

Let's say John's mom was always friendly and her house was
a good place to hang out. Fine. But the moment you go to her for
advice about getting a job, she's going to look at you a little bit
differently. She's going to size you up the way a potential
employer might. That's to say, if she *does* know someone who
has a position open and she's thinking of recommending you,
she's going to try to see you through her colleague's eyes. After

all, her own credibility will be on the line if she recommends you for a position in her field.

So even if you've known John's mom for years, even if she's seen you through your adolescence, it's now time to act professional.

What is she going to be looking for?

Evidence that you can present yourself well. Some indication that you can dress appropriately and speak maturely and respectfully and that you know how to prepare yourself for an interview by arming yourself with intelligent questions and concerns.

What kinds of questions?

Well, do some research to find out. Familiarize yourself with the field as much as you can by reading up on it on the Internet or in a bookstore or library. Then, having made it clear to the person you're "interviewing" that you have already done some legwork on your own, ask:

"Can you tell me a bit more about the profession?"

"What's the typical career path?"

"Do you find it gratifying?"

"Do you think it might be right for me?"

And then, at the end, if your prospective mentor has been encouraging and it feels appropriate, you could say:

"Thanks so much. I hope that if you hear of an opportunity in the field and you think I might be a good fit, you'll let me know. I'd be so grateful."

You'll put it in your own words, of course, but you get the general idea. You've made it clear that you hope she'll keep you in mind, and yet you haven't put her on the spot.

I've already told you that your choice of college major won't make or break your job search. But how you behave with potential mentors and in your interviews *can*.

So. Some more rules of the road.

## On Dealing with Mentors

Why is someone a mentor? Generally because, as I've said, people like to help other people. But there are limits to how much anyone can give. Prospective mentors will generally feel most comfortable if clear boundaries are set and if you stay well within them.

In the case of your friend's mother, go into the meeting expecting some information and advice. Nothing more. If she wants to take it a step further—if she wants to connect you with someone she knows who might have an opening—she'll do so.

If you're going to try to meet with someone you don't know—say, one of John's mom's colleagues (or a school alumnus, or someone your college's career office recommended, or your spin instructor's sister-in-law), then it's best to request a meeting or phone conversation with specific boundaries. Indicate that you are merely seeking an informational interview. Think of it: If you suggest that you're looking for a job and she doesn't have one to offer, she may think that meeting with you is a waste of everyone's time. But most people will be happy to help if you say, "I'm just learning about the profession and just looking for information, and Ms. Smith suggested I contact you," or "We went to college together, and I found your name through the alumni office. I'm interested in a career in PR and wonder if we could meet in person for just 20 minutes, or by phone for 10?"

If you have the choice, set up a personal meeting rather than a phone call. You'll make a stronger impression in person.

∽

A few final points to keep in mind.

A mentor or interviewer is only one person. He has likes and dislikes that may not align perfectly with yours. If what he says about a career goes against your gut instincts, then you may want to seek out one or two other people in the field and ask them to meet with you as well. The goal is to learn as much as you can while remembering that *no one knows you better than you know yourself.* The best thing you can do is to gather lots of new information, let it bump up against what you already know, and then see how it feels and where it leads you.

*"Wait a minute. What if I leave an interview and still don't know? What if I still feel confused?"*

That's okay.

An informational interview may blow away the path you *thought* you'd follow and leave you feeling like you're right back where you started. But that's still progress. In fact, learning what's *not* right for you can save you months or even a year. Or you may make a decision after one inspiring informational interview and get 3 months into a career before you realize it's not your ideal match. That's fine, too. Making a decision partly on faith is something successful people do all the time. The key is to get busy, gather as much information as you can, meet as many people as possible, and trust that it will lead you places. (We'll talk more about this in Part 4, Perspective.)

◎⁊

One last thing: We all want to *know* we're doing the right thing.

Can we ever be 100 percent sure?

Sometimes.

But quite often in life, we have to take a step while still having doubts. We can always find lots of reasons to think *I should have done this* or *I could have done that,* but we have to advance in spite of those thoughts. That's just how life is. If you're standing still until you feel totally right about a move, you may end up waiting a long time, or forever.

The brave thing is to take action—*knowing* you'll still have some doubts.

Then remember to keep your eyes open and trust that, along the way, you'll adjust your path.

## INTERVIEWS

So you've got yourself an interview. Congratulations! Even if it's just an informational one—well done. It's a big deal.

I know a woman who's a headhunter for people who earn over $500,000 a year. Of course these candidates' résumés get them in the door in the first place, but she says she can tell if they're right for the job by the way they walk in, say hello, make eye contact, and sit down. She says that 90 percent of the time, her first impression sticks. Then she's in the position of having to be polite and sit through the interview, even when she knows that she won't be making that candidate an offer. Think about that: Those candidates may make more money than you ever have, but they're out of work, too. And they may not feel confident, either. Yet first impressions are key, wherever you find yourself in the process.

Let's start at the beginning.

When you win yourself an interview, any interview, informational or for a specific job, do yourself the favor of a lifetime and follow these simple rules.

Be on time.

Look professional.

Bring your résumé.

Turn off your phone.

Do listen. Don't interrupt.

Ask questions . . . but not too many.

Say thank you.

I'm not trying to sound like your mother, and I know that these instructions may sound obvious, but you'd be surprised by how many people blow it by failing to do one or all of the above.

So let's review.

## Be On Time

This is all about demonstrating that you're considerate of your interviewer. The working world is a busy place. If you show up even 5 minutes late and have kept your interviewer waiting, you will have given the impression that you believe your time is more valuable than his or hers.

Ideally, you should try to get there 5 to 10 minutes early. That way, you have time to sit in the lobby or reception area or, if you're meeting with an individual at her home, in your car or a nearby café to collect and organize your thoughts.

Rushing into an interview all sweaty and crazed because you were late (or almost late) lowers your odds of getting an offer.

So if you don't know where you're going, figure out how to get there in advance. Maybe even make a test run. Estimate how long it will take you—and then leave 45 minutes earlier. If you get held up in traffic or stuck on public transportation, you'll be glad you built in the extra time. And if you've done everything you possibly can to get there on time but some catastrophe occurs, call the interviewer (ideally before you're already late), explain why you're going to be late, and apologize for the inconvenience.

If he or she is no longer available and needs to reschedule the meeting, be as open and flexible as possible with your own calendar. Avoid saying that you'll get back to them—it doesn't make you sound important, it makes you sound arrogant. Try to reschedule right then and there. Otherwise, you may never get another appointment.

If we're talking about an informational interview that you requested, time is also of the essence. Keep in mind that you need to be as prompt leaving as you were arriving. If you asked for 10 minutes of someone's day, make it 10 minutes. That's a realistic amount of time for a phone interview. In person, a meeting will never be less than 20, so you can ask for that. If you're in someone's office, you don't want to keep looking at your watch, as that implies discomfort or boredom, but keep in mind that 20 minutes in an office goes fast, as does 10 minutes on the phone. Stick to the limit as much as you can, or, if the conversation seems naturally to be running longer, you can ask if they have a moment more. But don't keep extending it.

## Look Professional

There's no getting around it: You're going to be judged in part by your appearance. Even John's mother is going to judge you by your appearance when you go to her house to discuss PR. As her child's friend, you only needed to look like everyone else, but even an informational interview with someone you know requires that you pull yourself together a bit.

If you go to someone's office, of course, you should aim to dress the way people do in the profession you aspire to—and maybe even a bit more smartly. Sure, there are architects and agents and editors and Web site designers who, once they're reasonably successful in their jobs, can get away with wearing jeans to work, but you are not (yet) one of those people. Unless you're being interviewed for a job bartending at Jimmy's BBQ Bar & Grill, play it safe: Wear a suit and tie. If you're a woman, wear a suit or similarly professional-looking ensemble. If you're not sure how to dress, it's best to err on the side of overdressing. And a side note: If dressing the way that the people interviewing you dress feels too much like a compromise of your personal style and taste, then you might ask yourself whether the industry you're auditioning for is really one that will make you happy—because chances are, to be successful in it, you're going to have to dress that way every day.

Basically, don't blow an interview by messing up something as simple as getting dressed. Employers want to know that their employees can be trusted to make a good first impression. So if you're going to be invited to work for them—to be part of their company's image—you need to do just that.

## Bring Your Résumé

This is about being prepared.

I know, I know: The guy should already have a copy of your résumé because you e-mailed it to him 3 weeks ago. But employers are looking for people who can make their lives easier by anticipating their needs and fulfilling them. So when he starts mumbling, "Now, where did I put your . . . " and begins ruffling through the papers on his desk, you'll win big points by pulling a fresh, crisp copy of your résumé out of your folder or bag and handing it to him. It will spare him the rest of this awkward scramble, and it will show that you are the kind of person who always comes prepared.

And if you have a related portfolio or any other "props" you think might boost your candidacy—for example, if you're applying for a job in the art department of a magazine and you have copies of the magazine you designed in college, or if you're the aspiring copywriter who took a stab at writing some sample ad copy of your own—bring those, too. You don't need to show up with enough show-and-tell to deliver a dramatic monologue of your entire life, but do go with a few supporting materials that you're proud of if they are relevant to the job for which you've applied.

## Turn Off Your Phone

Seriously. If you leave it on and it interrupts your conversation, you'll come off as rude and unprofessional.

## Do Listen. Don't Interrupt.

Listening is an art. Think about it: When you listen attentively, you take in more than merely what's being said. You're actually learning about the person speaking. People like to be listened to. If you listen well, you're showing respect and implying that you're open to learning—a decisive factor in the mind of any prospective employer. In fact, if you're a good listener, chances are that an interviewer will feel good about you, perhaps without even knowing why.

Talking too much and, certainly, interrupting send the exact opposite message: that you're not open or truly interested. What if you feel you know where the interviewer's going at a certain point in the conversation? Well, you may be right or you may not be, but either way, sit back and let him or her speak. Cutting someone off because you think you know where they're going (or for any other reason) will give the impression that you are impatient, unreceptive to learning new things, and disrespectful. In other words, interrupting is a good way to blow it.

Have you ever heard of "mirroring"? It's a communication strategy that notes the following psychological truth: Communication is a dance, and people tend to dance at their preferred speed and in their preferred way.

What does dancing have to do with being interviewed?

Let me explain.

If your interviewer takes her time asking you a question and you respond with a rapid-fire answer, you take the conversation from a waltz to the tango in the blink of an eye. In other words, you accelerate the conversation's natural rhythm, which means that you and your conversation partner are no longer keeping pace with one another. You are no longer in sync. You have taken the lead, or stepped on her toes. The same applies to volume, tone of voice, and other factors. In fact, the next time you're having an effortless conversation with a good friend, take note of these factors—you are probably mirroring each other without any conscious effort. It's easy to dance with a familiar partner.

Mirroring can help create an invaluable quality in an interview: rapport. And the bottom line is, people hire and recommend people they like. People with whom they want to spend more time, and with whom they have an immediate rapport. Jerry Seinfeld once said that an important factor in whom he cast for the small parts on his show was "Would we want to hang out with this person on the set?"

Beyond your objective qualifications, you will be hired—or not hired—based on your "chemistry" with your interviewer. You want to come across as someone who is reasonably confident, poised, easy to understand and communicate with, and endowed with a personality and some intelligent curiosity.

## Ask Questions . . . But Not Too Many

As I said in the last section, your interviewer is running the interview. You must be respectful of her (or his) time and status. Do a bit of homework before you go; research the company and its field, and formulate some intelligent questions that show you've already given some thought to why you're there and what the place is all about.

Let your interviewer direct the interview. Let her ask you if you have any questions before you start rattling them off, and let her finish her questions before you start to answer them. (This goes along with not interrupting; see above.)

While you're asking your questions, be sure to make eye contact. If you feel that you need to keep an open notebook on your lap just in case you want to write anything down, that's fine—but try to take notes sparingly. You want to seem alert and focused and able to keep the important stuff in your head. If you spend half the interview bent over your notebook, scribbling furiously, you'll waste an opportunity to give your interviewer the chance to get to know *you*.

If she doesn't ask you if you have any questions, it's appropriate to say, when the interview seems to be coming to a close, "I have a couple of questions. Would it be all right if I asked them now?"

When I was starting out, I used to think it was best not to ask anything. That was how I'd let someone know I was agreeable and would do whatever was required. Yet in reality, that's also the way I'd behave if I had no real interest and was just planning to stick it out at this job until something better came along. A person who sits there and says nothing isn't making a good case for herself. The interviewer wants to know you're respectful, yes—but she also wants to know if you have any questions about what the company does, or what you'd be doing if you worked there.

However, you should also try to gauge your interviewer's patience. Don't ramble on for too long. And do *not* get too personal, about yourself or the person sitting opposite you.

Don't say, "I Googled you and saw that you teach Pilates on the weekends. I love Pilates!" That's inappropriate, and it's downright creepy. If your interviewer wants to talk about Pilates, *she'll* bring it up. And she definitely doesn't want to think about you Googling her.

And don't ask what the salary is before anyone has even offered you a job. If you get offered the job, you'll find out what it is. But if you ask, you probably won't be offered the job because, again, it will seem like you're jumping the gun.

*Do* feel free to make comments along these lines:

"I've been reading online about new customizable software that lots of PR companies are using. Is that something you're thinking about using here, too?"

Or:

"I've read that this firm has several Spanish clients, which interests me because I'm fluent in Spanish and I hope to be able to incorporate my language ability into my work."

Questions and comments like these show that you are interested in how the business works and how you might become a useful part of it.

And while it's fine to inquire modestly about opportunities for growth within the company, do not make it seem as though you would be doing your potential employer a *favor* by working there. This may sound obvious, but you'd be surprised by how many people don't get an offer because they come across as having the wrong attitude. Employers like eagerness—so long as it's eagerness to learn and work hard, not eagerness to be promoted right after the starting bell. Your interviewer needs to feel comfortable with your expectations. For example, she doesn't want to hear or think that there are certain things you just won't do. If she picks up that vibe, she'll just move on to the next person. It's good to appear confident, but you also need to communicate that you're willing to *earn* your progress up the ranks—starting from square one. In many cases, this means not being allergic to small tasks like answering phones

or performing needed clerical work well. Not that you neces
sarily need to *say* that you're interested in doing such tasks as a
part of your job, but try not to imply that you think you're
above them.

Don't worry. Entry level won't last forever.

The key, at this point, is to get your foot in the door.

## Say Thank You

And not just on your way out the door. I mean in writing.

Briefly thanking your interviewer in writing for her time is
essential. Trust me. People appreciate notes. Why? Because it's
an extension of knowing how to say please and thank you. People appreciate being appreciated. And notes reinforce, again,
that you're professional and you value other people's time.

It can also be a way to show that you don't have unrealistic
expectations. You're acknowledging what she's already done,
while simultaneously laying down terms to keep the contact
alive.

So send an e-mail a few hours later. It is a tangible sign of
your character and willingness to go the distance.

If you met briefly with a potential mentor, just for some
information, your e-mail might look like this.

Dear Ms. Murphy:

I was referred to you by Mary Jones and just wanted
to thank you again for seeing me yesterday.

Your advice reinforced my interest in working in
public relations and also gave me several good ideas
regarding how I should proceed. You mentioned that a
former colleague of yours at Acme Public Relations

might be looking for an assistant—I'd be extremely grateful if you'd be willing to pass my name along or let me know whether and how I might contact the person myself.

I very much appreciated our informative and enjoyable meeting. What a pleasant surprise to learn that you're originally from Seattle, as well! I hope to remain in touch, and I wish you the best.

Sincerely,

Sarah Thompson

This is just a sample, of course. Ideally in *your* note you would touch upon each of the following: how you made the connection, what you gained, what your goals are, and something—anything—to personalize it, to make it unique and fresh.

But keep it to less than a page. You want it to be a pleasure to receive and read, not an imposition.

And if you think your new contact might be open to staying in touch with you, you can contact her again a few weeks later. But don't just write, "Hi, I wonder whether you have any new leads for me?" A good way to get back in touch is to bring new information to the table, to let your generous mentor know the various ways in which *you're* relevant: perhaps briefly noting a point you've observed in the news and how it relates to her company/the industry, or telling her how you've been busy trying to find a job, rather than just waiting for her to do something for you.

A thank-you note to someone who interviewed you for a specific position should look more like this.

Dear Ms. Green:

I just wanted to thank you formally for seeing me yesterday.

Speaking with you reinforced my interest in working in this field—and learning more about Paulson Public Relations has made me extremely enthusiastic about the possibility of working with you specifically. Finding the right words and ways to disseminate stories strategically is something I feel very passionate about. I also enjoyed your stories about Madrid and was grateful for the opportunity to brush up on my Spanish!

So thank you again, and please do let me know if I can provide you with any additional information that may aid my candidacy. I would be greatly honored to join your team, and I hope to hear from you soon.

Meanwhile, I wish you all the best.

Sincerely,

Sarah Thompson

That's all. Keep it short, sweet, and respectful. And if you have any doubts, ask someone smart and honest to help you write it, or to proofread it for you before you press send.

*"Okay, Ken. I've been following all your advice for weeks now, I've been networking and talking to mentors and going to interviews and writing thank-you notes, and* I still don't have a job. *Got any other ideas?"*

Yes. I do.

Turn the page.

CHAPTER 5

# WHAT ABOUT INTERNSHIPS? VOLUNTEERING?

Make yourself necessary to somebody.

—RALPH WALDO EMERSON

USUALLY, A PAYING, FULL-TIME JOB is preferable to an internship or volunteer work. But it's an especially competitive job market out there right now, and more often than not, people don't get a job right away. Or, to get the job they want, they may need more experience. In this case, an internship or volunteer position can be a good way to get your foot in the door, make contacts, stay active, and maybe even wind up being paid.

I can already hear the response:

*"But most internships don't pay. And volunteering definitely doesn't pay!"*

True. But in order to perk up your résumé, it may be that the right strategy for the next few months is to maximize the benefits of a nonpaying position and scramble a bit. Sure, it might require living with your parents for the summer, or continuing to live with them for longer than you'd planned to, or sharing a one-bedroom apartment with two roommates. You may even need to work early mornings in a coffee shop or bartend at night to cover your expenses.

But if in exchange you get some real experience and make contacts in the field you know or think will interest you, it could be well worth it.

Maybe you want to break into publishing, and a literary magazine you love offers a great internship in which you actually get to read the short story submissions that come in and decide which ones the editor in chief should consider.

Or maybe you're an aspiring programmer, or you want to work in Web site marketing. In either case, an internship with a search engine or social networking site could be just the thing.

Or maybe you're interested in environmental science, and you're applying for jobs that have to do with environmental education. And in the meantime, it will boost your résumé, not to mention keep the positive energy flowing, if you volunteer at your local nature conservancy a few afternoons each week.

That said, there are internships and there are *internships*. There's volunteering and there's *volunteering*. You don't want to scramble financially for a nonpaying "opportunity" that's a waste of your time.

So how do you separate the good ones from the bad?

A man once raised his hand at one of my talks. He'd graduated with a film degree and was wondering whether to take an internship at a small film production company in New York. He told me he'd already done the same type of thing before, and he wasn't very excited to do it a second time, but nothing else had come along.

I pointed out that in the film business, virtually anyone can own a "production company." If my wife and I decided we wanted to make a film, even a really bad film, we could incorporate ourselves and voilà! We'd be in the movie business. Our home would be our headquarters.

In this guy's previous internship with a small company, his duties involved:

Sitting in the owners' living room.

Occasionally answering the phone.

Making coffee. Sometimes twice a day.

On Fridays, picking up the owners' dry cleaning.

And now he was wondering whether to do the same type of thing again, just to stay busy, and for the résumé credit.

Here's the thing: If this guy, having interned for Hanger/ Light-Starch Productions and thus being unable to put a single film-related activity on his résumé, took his résumé down to Miramax and showed it to human resources, HR would take one look at it and probably peg him as the type who has experience answering phones, making coffee, and fetching dry cleaning. Which is fine—but not exactly a fast track to the Academy Awards.

The HR department would know that the duties of an intern at a fledgling production company are similar to those of an employee in an entry-level position at an established company. Which, again, is fine. Answering phones, making coffee, and, yes, shuttling dry cleaning are the dues people pay when they start out in many an industry. You saw *The Devil Wears Prada,* right?

But at least in an entry-level position you'd be getting paid.

So when is an unpaid internship or volunteer position a good idea?

When:

- It helps you establish valuable connections within the industry.
- It teaches you something constructive.
- It helps you feel upbeat and productive.
- It might actually turn into a paying position.

(It's true; some of them do.)

These are the criteria you should be considering if you are considering working for free. If the internship meets any or all of these objectives, it may be worth your (unpaid) time.

Needless to say, I told the man at my talk that if collecting laundry and making coffee and answering phones in someone's living room was the full extent of the internship, *and* he wasn't looking forward to the experience, *and* there was no chance it might turn into a paying job, he shouldn't take it.

But if an internship offers some actual hands-on experience doing any of the things studio execs or even creative types do— fund-raising, scouting for filming locations, reading scripts, auditioning actors, navigating distribution channels, hiring film editors and lighting designers, or applying to the festival cir- cuit—well now, *that's* a different story. Even if it's a small com- pany (even if it's a dinky little production company) but you, the intern, *will* be personally involved in film-industry activities such as these, and (better yet), if this company actually produces films you respect and admire, then even if it is run out of a living room, it's still a good thing. It gives you *a lot* to put on your résumé and talk about during your Miramax interview.

In fact, smaller companies are sometimes ideal places to gain experience because they don't have as many people to do the important tasks. That means quite a few of the important tasks fall to . . . you guessed it. The intern. You.

And remember, if you take an internship and on the first day the only thing you're asked to do is answer the phone, that doesn't mean you should call it quits. People will test you at first to make sure you are trustworthy enough to eventually handle bigger tasks. Which brings us to another point: Even if the tasks that are assigned to you feel trivial, silly, or downright insulting—if you don't do them well, and with a good attitude, you're never going to be offered more substantial responsibilities. Give it a little time.

If, after a couple of weeks, you see things you think you could do, ask your supervisor if you can roll up your sleeves and pitch in. Envision the task list that would look great on your résumé, and then offer to do those things. This is the beauty of internships and volunteer opportunities: Because you're not being paid, you can actually be a little creative about your position. You can make it what *you* want it to be, provided you seek permission first.

Sometimes the people who've "hired" you won't be great managers. Sometimes they'll be so busy doing their own jobs that assigning you interesting work won't come naturally to them. So help them out. Look around. Ask yourself, "What can I do to help the organization get organized and also familiarize myself with some new aspects of the industry?"

If we're still talking about the film industry, you could sort through the slush pile (the unsolicited scripts) and pick out the ones you think the company should consider producing and the ones to which it should say, "Thanks, but no thanks." Or you could offer to make a list of all the film festivals taking place in North America within the next 6 months. Or you could offer to draft an online ad for the sound editor the company needs so desperately.

Provided you are doing something good for the enterprise, and provided you don't interfere with your boss's ability to perform her own job on time, she will appreciate your initiative.

Finally, it's understood that you'll list volunteer experiences and internships on your résumé, but *don't think twice* about being proud to talk about those experiences in interviews. A potential employer won't be overly concerned with the fact that you weren't paid; her main goal in the interview is to figure out who you are and what kind of experience you're bringing to the table.

Let her know.

☙

*OK, Ken, I'm sold. Internships and volunteering sound great—but I can't afford to work for free!*

Here's another idea:

Temping.

Temping is sort of like a series of little "surprise" internships: You get to see lots of different work environments and gain short-term experience fast—but you also get paid. If there's a temping agency near you, apply to be put on their roster of people available to fill in last-minute for full-time employees who call in sick or go on maternity leave or whatever. One day you might find yourself answering phones at an architecture firm, another day typing letters for a lawyer—and, you never know: If you hit it off with someone senior at one of these companies, one of those temp jobs might very well turn into a permanent position. It happens. At the very least, you'll add a few lines to your résumé, learn more about your likes and dislikes, *and* walk away with a bit more money in your pocket at the end of the day.

In short: There are two tricks to making the most of internships, volunteer opportunities, or temping: 1) affording to work for little or no money, maybe by living at home or with some roommates, and taking on a part-time paying job to make ends meet, and 2) making the work, whatever it is, *work for you.*

# CHAPTER 6

# FINDING YOUR PASSION

Learn to read your own mind and
everything else will come by itself.

—PAUL VALÉRY

I KNOW A MAN WHO'S a well-known architect in New York City
and Paris. When he was 54, he read some of my career advice,
written for twenty-something grads. "Ken," he said, "I loved
it—because I'm still trying to figure out what to do with my
life."

He was kidding.

But not 100 percent kidding. Not 80 percent kidding. Maybe
51 percent kidding.

The truth is this: Figuring out what you really, really want
to do is an ongoing process, not an event. Some people have an
idea of what their passion is before they begin the job search.
Others have to figure it out along the way. But for most people,
it's a process of continual refinement. It involves knowing, not
knowing, knowing again, and—on occasion—going all the way
back to the drawing board.

So whether you're in a phase of knowing, of feeling clueless,
or of actually being in a job but still trying to figure it out, a few
techniques for finding your passion can help.

## TECHNIQUE I: TRIGGER QUESTIONS

Ask yourself:

"What would I do if money weren't an issue?"

"What do I think needs to be done?"

"How can I be useful? Helpful? Constructive?"

"What areas of life have value and meaning for me?" "Wait a minute," you might say. "This is a waste of time. I don't feel passionate about anything."

But we all have passions. Yes, even you.

Sometimes they're invisible because they get covered. Blocked by years of *information*—schoolwork, Web sites, and TV—jamming your brain. Your true passions can also get blocked by other people's ideas. Passions tend to run away from the "shoulds," by which I mean what you and other people think you *should* do, for whatever reason.

But asking yourself these questions—really considering them—will help you shut out the noise that might otherwise distract you from figuring it out.

Figuring what out, exactly?

What you could do, and be paid to do, that would also make you happy.

Start with whichever question feels most relevant right now, or take them one at a time.

## What would I do for free?

Your first answer may be "Lie on the beach."

I get it. But unless you want to be a lifeguard (and maybe you do, which is fine—the world needs lifeguards!), we need to keep going. The first answers you think of aren't always the ones that will point you in a good direction—they can even be discouraging.

Let's refine the question a little:

"What would I do for free that would also add value on some level?"

Or it may be easier to think about it this way:

"If I were going to volunteer, what would I do?"

The first answer may sound like this: "I'd help people."

Or maybe "I'd work with children."

"I'd build houses for those in need."

But it's better to try to make it more specific.

Would you teach?

Coach?

Work with your hands?

Address a societal problem, like poverty or minority rights?

Let's say Sam has no desire to volunteer—but if she did, she'd help people learn to read, because she loves to read. But still, this makes no sense to her as a career strategy because she's a business major and she's looking for a job in sales.

Of course, there are definite connections to be made: For one, she could sell programs or products that help promote literacy. But she doesn't need to go there yet, because there may be much bigger connections that will come more naturally later.

For now, Sam's just trying to get more information on who she really is, what makes her tick.

Think of three areas in which you would be willing to volunteer. Make them as specific as you can.

Write them down, even if they're just random notes and observations. Why? The act of writing things down helps you begin to record these small pieces of the puzzle in your mind, and your mind will take them further on its own, sometimes even without any additional conscious input. Over time, your brain may connect the dots *for* you.

Once you've written down your thoughts, ask yourself: "Did my ideas for volunteering involve working with people or things?"

For example, helping someone read is working with people. But if you were going to restore a building, it's working with a thing, even if it's ultimately *for* people's use.

More questions about your volunteering ideas:

Do they take place indoors or outdoors?

Do they involve big organizations or small ones?

Normal, 9-to-5 working hours or irregular ones?

Working on teams or alone?

Sam's idea might give her the following information: She's interested in literacy, she enjoys working with people, she likes working indoors, and she likes regular working hours.

This information doesn't necessarily tell her *exactly* what her dream job is, but it may give her the first pieces of the puzzle.

*"But, Ken, what if I'm having a really hard time coming up with even three types of volunteer work I'd be willing to do?"*

Write down "Three places I'd volunteer?" in a notebook or on your computer or on your phone. Let the question just sit there for a while, as a placeholder, and trust that your mind will work on this on its own.

Seriously. You may wake up one day knowing where you'd volunteer, or, just as likely, your mind will start to ask itself: *What makes me tick? What would I do for free? Where would*

*I volunteer?* And gradually it will suggest more and more specific ideas along the lines of *What's "right" for me?* It won't happen entirely consciously, which is why you can't always push it; the process involves your senses and, yes, moods and even dreams.

Let's say you couldn't come up with a volunteering idea, so you just wrote down or sent yourself a text message asking, "Where would I volunteer?" and went to the gym.

Then, while driving home later, you passed a park, and you saw people repainting the fence. Falling asleep that night, you found yourself thinking, *Okay. That's a possibility. Maybe if I were going to volunteer, I'd help fix up a park.*

Or maybe you had a dream of yourself painting a fence in a park.

Then, 3 weeks later, or maybe even months later, while working at a bike shop or some entry-level office job just to pay your rent, you suddenly think, *Wait a minute! What about landscape architecture?*

Do landscape architects paint fences? Well, probably at some point in their lives, though the job is much more than that. But do you see how the process can work? Having planted the question "What would I do for free?" in your mind, you made yourself more aware of the possibilities. And when you saw some people sprucing up an outdoor space, this, too, planted a seed, which led you to an even more promising possibility: designing and sprucing up outdoor spaces *for a living.*

So at this point, if you aren't able to crank out a list of ways in which you'd love to work for free, you just need to *seed your mind.* That means planting ideas—or rather, not the ideas themselves, but little bits of information, real or symbolic, about what kinds of activities might be right for you—so that the ideas can grow.

## What do I think needs to be done?

Your initial thoughts may run along the lines of *People need to take care of each other* or *People need to look out for each other.*

Those are fine places to start, but they'll give you much more direction if you can make them more specific.

*How* do people need to take care of each other?

"Well," you say, "communities should be safer."

Okay. Then maybe you think, *More policemen.*

Maybe *you* want to be a policeman!

Or . . . maybe you don't.

In which case, ask yourself: "Where would more policemen come from? Who would pay them? Who would train them?"

And then you think, *Politics. Political policy. Politicians (in theory) often decide whether expanding a police force is necessary.*

Great progress! Write all this down!

It doesn't have to be an epic novel. Your notes can just look something like this:

- People taking care of each other
- Safer towns
- Police
- Politics

Leave room at the bottom for whatever else comes to you—tomorrow, maybe, or not until next week, or next month. You probably won't figure this out in a day or even a week, but the trick is to get into the process.

Again, right now, you're just planting seeds.

For another person, the notes may begin with something much more specific. Imagine that Rachel comes up with this: "People need to eat healthier foods."

Which might then prompt her to write:

Educate them . . . how? Magazines, Web sites, coaching . . .

Increase their access to affordable, nutritious, high-quality foods.

Make those foods more appealing!

Already, Rachel has hit upon a gold mine of possible job prospects for someone interested in promoting healthy eating. Though she may not yet realize it, her notes can lead her, or any competent career counselor, to:

Writer or editor of a health magazine, newsletter, or Web site

Personal diet coach

Employee or owner of a health food store

Employee or founder of a public advocacy group that promotes healthy eating

Policy maker, fund-raiser, or administrator for the FDA

Nutritionist

Healthy foods restaurateur, chef, or recipe-book writer

But the notes come first.

All of these possibilities are ways in which Rachel can be useful, helpful, and constructive—while doing something related to one of her interests.

No one is going to pay you simply to do what you love. Generally, people pay other people to be useful, helpful, entertaining, inspiring, or otherwise positively contributive to the world in some way. Your goal is to find the thing (or things) that you love *and* that fit into the contributive category. A professional golfer isn't paid simply to play golf: She's paid to play golf exceptionally well—which is entertaining and makes money for advertisers. And a professional magazine writer isn't paid simply to write: He's paid to write something that other people want to read, whether that's because it's informative, entertaining, inspiring, revealing, or beautiful, or any of the above—provided it contributes to a magazine's sales.

Maybe Rachel isn't passionate about healthy food, but maybe she is passionate about cooking and experimenting with new recipes, so by combining the "need" she has identified with something she feels passionate about, she might have stumbled onto a few ideas for potentially fulfilling careers—as a policy maker, nutritionist, or cookbook editor.

How can you be useful, helpful, or constructive?

*"I'd be useful if I had enough money to pay the rent."*

I know. We'll get there, because having enough money to get by is critical. But for now, stay with me.

How can you be useful? How can you be helpful?

Say Alex's parents got divorced, and he was devastated. But the experience has given him a lot of empathy and understanding that allow him to help other people he meets who are going through their own parents' divorces. That's how he feels useful, and he even enjoys it, because the people appreciate his advice and seem to benefit from it.

He also likes the idea of being his own boss.

So he decides that he might enjoy, and be good at, being a therapist. Helping other people get through difficult family situations, using both his own experiences and what he would learn in the right training program or PhD track. That's how he'd help others—and be paid for it.

## What areas of life have value and meaning for me?

Maybe you love poetry. Or jazz. Or philosophical arguments. Or nature.

Maybe you love democracy, or the Constitution.

Maybe you love photography.

Or gardening.

Or your family.

Or your ethnic or religious heritage.

Make a list. If the words *value* and *meaning* seem too abstract and are tripping you up, forget about them for now.

Just fill in this blank, over and over again, without thinking about jobs or careers: "I love _____."

Try to list at least five things.

Look around your room, or think of all the things you did in the past week, or month, or year, for ideas.

Then, try plugging some of them, maybe in slightly different forms, into the blanks below, and see what you get.

Editor, designer, or technical support provider for new media _____ Web site, magazine, or newsletter

Personal _____ coach, therapist, or guide

Marketing or PR director for _____

Employee or founder of a _____ coalition or nonprofit/public advocacy group

Policy maker, fund-raiser, or administrator for the _____ _____ Administration

_____ teacher or professor at the primary school, high school, university, or continuing education level

Obviously you'll have to play around with the words a little bit, but you get the gist. There's no such thing as a "Philosophical Arguments Administration," but there *is* an American Philosophical Association, an American Philosophical Society, and an International Association for Philosophy and Literature—and organizations like these need people to run and represent them.

There's no such thing (to my knowledge) as an "American Constitution Store," but there is the possibility of becoming a lawyer who defends the Constitution or becoming a teacher who educates young people about it.

"Personal Italian Heritage Therapist" sounds a bit silly, I know, but how can we tweak it so it becomes something that both taps into your interest in your family's background and is of value to other people? Maybe you love to cook Italian food, or speak Italian, or look at Italian art, or visit Italian cities. Could you teach other people about those things? Could you research or write for an Italian travel guide, or customize Italian travel itineraries, or give private Italian lessons to children, or be the manager of an Italian café?

*"Ken! Stop it! I'm not Italian! I don't know anything about Italy!"*

That's fine. Just go back to your own list, pick one thing that has value and meaning for you—that you love—and play around with how to plug versions of that thing into this list. Keep working down the list of things you love, and I promise you your mind will begin to open up.

# TECHNIQUE II: DETECTIVE WORK AND LATERAL THINKING

Finding your passion is an ongoing job. It's something you'll keep coming back to, rather than something you just "figure out" in one try. So here's another method; it involves detective work in the form of lateral thinking.

*"Lateral wha-a-a?"*

Stay with me.

Say I ask you, "What do you like to do?"

And you respond, "Listen to music."

Okay. I'm aware that "listening to music" might just be code for "Stop asking these questions and leave me alone. I just want to listen to music." But let's assume you really do like listening to music and you want to consider how this might clue you in to what you should "do with your life."

There are some obvious possibilities.

Musician
Club owner
DJ
Producer

But say none of these seem right, either. You're not a musician. You don't like clubs. You don't like public speaking. And to be a music producer, you'd need a lot more money to throw around.

So, what now?

You could be a music agent.

That's not a bad idea. In fact, some of you will run with it.

But maybe the more you think about it, the more you realize

that music's your favorite thing to do, period. You don't want to work with it. You just love listening to it.

Okay. That's fine.

But how is "I like listening to music" still useful?

Well, let's see. What is it that you like about listening to music?

Music is art. It's creative.

It's aesthetic. Good music inspires people to see beauty in other things, which enhances the quality of life in general.

Is it possible another aesthetic field might do the same for you?

Let's call music "creative content." People who produce bands or jazz groups or classical musicians *choose creative content.*

That's the tricky part: coming up with the label. But it gets easier after a little practice.

Okay. So, who else chooses creative content?

What about literary agents?

Think about it: They do for books what the music company people do for music. And I don't even mean an agent who represents books about music (although you could pursue that avenue, too). I just mean that "I like listening to music" can logically lead you to ask, "Would I like to be a literary agent?"

That's the whole art of lateral thinking. Learning to take an idea from one area to another.

Let's take it further. Maybe now you're thinking:

*Literary agents read manuscripts. That sounds like fun. But that can't be all there is to being a literary agent. What else do they do?*

Then you ask around, check the Internet, or experience

divine intervention, and you discover that literary agents represent authors.

- They match them up with publishers.
- They negotiate deals and contracts.

Oops. Maybe you're out at this point, if that doesn't sound interesting to you.

But what if, yes, you still like it?

You might be thinking, *It would be cool to represent talented people.*

To match them up with other people.

To strike deals on their behalf.

So let's keep it going. How can we laterally expand that one?

Put on your detective's hat and ask, "Who else represents talented people and makes big deals?"

Other kinds of agents.

What kinds?

Actors' agents.

Artists' agents.

Photographers' agents.

Okay, when you're sitting at home, I don't expect you to just reel them off as I did here. Because frankly, these didn't just come to me in a flash of inspiration. I had to take some time and think of them.

But if you say a literary agent represents talent, keep asking yourself, "Who else does?"

How about . . . a sports agent?

There you go!

Just by moving laterally, trying to make connections, you've come all the way from "I like listening to music" to "Maybe I'd enjoy being a sports agent."

And now, if "sports agent" interests you, the thing to do would be to check it out online. Learn a little more. If what you find there continues to hold your interest, you could try to arrange an informational interview with an alum of your school who's a sports agent—or, if you liked the sound of another kind of agent better, whichever kind you have in mind.

Now you're actually giving *yourself* a meeting. This will help you continue to get better at meetings and better at presenting yourself. And, of course, you'll be vetting the idea to find out if it's truly one that might be right for you.

So you call an alum or send an e-mail. And, gulp, now you're waiting for him to reply.

More waiting! Grrrr.

But you can jump-start the process by finding a professional association or a seminar for sports agents.

It sounds like a slow road—for some, the mere idea of a professional association sounds boring—but a seminar, or a meeting at an association, or a mentor you find through the professional association can take you places. Into "Yes, this sounds right for me, at least as a starting point for a first job" or, just as valuable, "No, it's not quite the thing."

In the process, you may learn about another avenue you hadn't thought of. Taking action often leads you to receive new information.

But even if it's a false start, it's positive movement, because you're building a bigger framework of "who I am and what might be right."

Let's stay with this one a little longer.

"You know what?" you say. "I've thought about this a little bit more, and an agent is a businessperson, which I'm not."

Okay. But let's go back to your interest in music, to see what other ideas come up.

So now we have to consider not the *business* of music, but music itself.

Think again about why you like listening to music.

Maybe you like how music affects you on emotional levels. It helps you relax and dream. It changes the way you feel. Sometimes you start out sad and end up happy. Sometimes you start out happy and end up sad. Maybe you like its emotional power.

Okay. Now, to generalize.

How about emotional power?

Nah. It doesn't suggest anything obvious.

How about this: Music leads to *changing states*. Not moving from New Hampshire to Oregon, but changes in the state of your body and mind.

Sound good?

Let's go with it.

What else changes the states of our bodies and minds?

Let's see. There's exercise.

Then we think about it longer and come up with more.

Meditation.

Therapy.

Okay. Do these suggest any careers?

Maybe you would like to be a coach?

A yoga teacher?

A trainer?

A mental or physical therapist?

Again, even if none of these lateral jumps gets you going, just keep writing down any that come close or seem interesting to you. You can revisit the list later, just to see whether it looks a little bit different after some time has passed.

So now, text yourself or write down, "Changes the way I feel."

Yoga teacher?

*No.*

Therapist?

Hey, therapist has possibilities.

∽

What if you aspire to a career in finance? You visualize yourself helping people to value assets, like stocks, bonds, and commodities. But maybe you need an advanced degree to break into that (or even to learn what commodities are!). And while deciding whether or not to pursue the degree—and as you research what's involved—perhaps you want to consider some related fields that you may enjoy. You might even see if you can incorporate other interests.

What else could we call this?

How about "evaluating financial assets"?

The next question: "How else do people value financial assets?"

What about those who invest in real estate? Or estate planners?

Any others?

If none come to mind, we can change it. How about dropping the word *financial,* so we have "evaluating assets."

Let's see. There are people who value and invest in wine futures. Art auctioneers. Or even the credit side of the casino business.

Do any of these interest you? If not, that's helpful knowledge, and you can keep going. Perhaps you'd change the word *evaluating* to one that may spark new ideas. Or maybe one of those listed above might interest you just enough to explore it further—to talk to people in the field. Perhaps the next move for you is to learn more about this variation on "finance" and use it as your stepping-stone to business school, which will deliver you to a new form of finance—if that's where you want to be.

The trick is to expand the scope of possibilities.

I don't expect you to be an instant expert at lateral thinking, or to be able to instantly fabricate phrases like "changing states" or "choosing creative content." And I don't expect you to land on your dream career within 5 minutes—although some of you might.

For now, I just want to introduce the idea and ask you to start playing with it in your mind. The art is not merely making labels, but figuring yourself out.

The clues come from what you like to do.

Here are some other questions to consider.

What are you talented at doing?

What were you doing when you were happiest?

When were you most effective?

Let's start with that last one—when were you most effective?

The answer to this question doesn't have to come from a professional context. Alex might say, "When my parents were having problems, I used to help them out. I mediated between them, and it sometimes kept the peace."

Okay. Interesting.

Now ask yourself: What might that suggest about who you are?

What you're good at?

What comes naturally to you?

And this brings us to . . .

## TECHNIQUE III: THE VERBS

"When my parents were having problems, I used to help them out. I *mediated* between them."

Think of that in terms of verbs. What skills might this suggest that you have?

Let's see: *mediating*, for one.

(And that's just the first one that comes to mind.)

Write it down. *Mediating*.

What else?

Think about when you've had to mediate between your parents. What else were you doing? Look for the gerunds, the active "-ing" words.

Maybe peacemaking.

*Negotiating*.

Good.

Now let's think of a happier time, like the time you organized a surprise birthday party for your sister. You took care of collecting donations from friends and then did all the inviting and cooking and decorating yourself.

You were *planning*.

Then you think some more, and maybe later or the next day you'll find yourself adding to the list.

*Fund-raising.*

*Catering.*

*Decorating.*

A few days later you might add *socializing*.

And what about the time your best friend asked you for advice about her boyfriend?

In fact, now that you think about it, friends are always coming to you for advice.

So go on. The verbs?

*Advising.*

*Problem solving.*

*Empathizing.*

In this way—by thinking about your experiences and the verbs associated with them—you can make your own list. Then sit back and ask yourself whether it looks to you like a good sampling of your skills.

Then think about what careers those verbs might suggest.

The lists above suggest hundreds of possibilities having to do with law, psychology, diplomacy, catering, social planning, fund-raising, design, and business.

*"But wait a minute,"* you say. *"I'm not sure I want to use some of these skills. After all, I hated when I was put in the position of figuring things out for my parents. That's the last thing I want to do at work."*

That's fine! You've still learned something from your list. Maybe until now you were thinking, *I should probably just go to law school and become a lawyer.* But maybe the reason you hated being in the middle of your parents' quarrels was because you hate mediating—even if you *are* good at it. It frustrates you. It stresses you out. It makes you angry. And maybe, just possibly, now that you've arrived at this little revelation, you should consider ruling out law school.

So it's good to know who you are and to be on the lookout for these kinds of clues. One good method is to keep a list called Verbs, and when you're out with friends, or waiting for a movie to begin, or in the park, ask yourself: "What verbs am I? Which ones describe the things I do well?"

Keep an eye out for the skills you exercise naturally in the course of each day. Identify the verbs and write them down. Eventually, when you have some time to spend online or at the career center, see if you can identify a few jobs that make use of those verbs in ways that appeal to you and fit your skill set (the one that is transferable, remember?).

One way to warm up is by making a list of the verbs you observe in people. Friends. People you admire. Famous people.

David Letterman. What does he do? What are his verbs?

He's a comedian. An interviewer. A storyteller. A social commentator.

The verbs: Satirizing. Interviewing. Storytelling. Commentating.

The president. What does he do? What are his verbs?

He runs things. Thinks of (useful) policies, seeks popular support, and works with Congress to adopt them.

The verbs: Leading. Managing. Problem solving. Mediating. Inspiring.

Now, back to you:

What was your favorite childhood memory?

Or, what's the thing of which you're most proud?

*"I was on the debate team."*

Debating! Great. That suggests politics, law, and journalism, for starters.

*"And the team I coached made it to the hockey finals."*

Competing! Coaching! Being part of a team! More aptitudes that come in handy in all sorts of areas.

If you love competing, or the excitement of competition, maybe you belong in professional sports, or sales, or advertising.

If you like coaching, maybe you should look at careers that involve leading and motivating groups.

And if you like being part of a team, that implies that you might be happy in organizations where you'd collaborate with others, rather than in a profession where you'd primarily work alone.

Though The Verbs is the third technique, it may be the easiest way for you to start. Start asking yourself, "What verb am I right now? What verb was I when I was happiest in the last week?" Then you can plug what you learn here into the other techniques. The order you try these in is interchangeable.

Finally, remember that figuring out what you want to do is a *process*, not something that happens in an instant. It's common to read exercises like the ones I listed above, grab your pen and a sheet of paper, and find yourself overwhelmed. As in: *How am I supposed to make a label? Or think of myself as a verb? And even if I think of one, then what?* It's important to remember during those frustrating moments that you're trying to uncover some fundamental information. Your mind may resist at first—that's common. If that happens, just start slowly. Even if you just write down a fragment and have to stop there and put down the pen and paper, you've made a start. The key is to come back to it when you're ready and to add a little more. You might choose to start fresh each time, or you may build on what you've already started. That's how the process works.

It's going to involve trial and error. But it can also be fun, figuring it out and learning about yourself along the way. The really interesting thing is this: On some level, you probably do already know what you're looking for. But, as I've said, it can get covered up by "stuff"—like ideas of what you *should* do, rather than what you want to do, what will make you feel engaged and alert and fulfilled.

Use these techniques to clear away any obstacles and to spark your inner flame. They'll ultimately lead you to uncover your passions.

# CHAPTER 7

# SURVIVING ENTRY LEVEL

*A positive attitude may not solve all your problems, but it will
annoy enough people to be worth the effort.*

—HERM ALBRIGHT

SO HERE YOU ARE, COLLEGE degree in hand, and you find yourself . . . in a little cubicle crunching numbers. Or being asked to
answer the phone.

Grrr.

What now?

If you're like many people, "the gremlins" take center
stage.

What are the gremlins? Those little voices in our heads. You
know, the ones that make us feel worse.

Let me introduce you to the entry-level gremlins. There's
one over there! Let's say hello.

YOU: Hi there, Gremlin. How are you?

GREMLIN: You're doing the wrong thing!

YOU: Huh? What are you talking—

GREMLIN: You're in the wrong job and the wrong field.

Gulp!

That wasn't very friendly, was it? Well, nice to meet you, too!

Let's talk to another one. One way to initiate conversation is to talk about a neutral subject, such as the weather.

YOU: Excuse me, Gremlin? Nice weather we're having, isn't it?

GREMLIN: I have only one thing to say to that.

YOU: Yes?

GREMLIN: You're going to be stuck in that @#$%! job of yours for the rest of your life!

YOU: What?!

GREMLIN: You'll be here, in this horrible job, forever. *Why did you even bother going to college at all?*

Whoa!

You see? Now you know who the gremlins are and what they do. And the worst part, of course, is that they live *in your head.*

So how do you battle them?

Consider this: So long as you're telling yourself that you're stuck, you're stuck. It's an old psychological truism. We play a major part in our own perceptions of the world around us.

*"Perceptions? But maybe the gremlins are right! I didn't go to college to get coffee and make copies."*

Okay, I'll say it another way: Entry level is challenging, but you're not helpless.

☙

Let's start there. How do you take control of your entry-level position?

By understanding that it's the starting point, the front door—and that there are ways to try to maximize the experience.

There's no getting around it. You just had 4 years of college, more or less living on your own schedule, and now you find yourself in what feels like prison.

Why do you have to endure it? Why is entry level the starting point? Well, frankly, no one's going to let you start at the top. People by nature are competitive and territorial, by which I mean protective of their own achievements—as they should be. If you spent 10 years paying your dues—working your way up to a nice office, a good salary, and more interesting responsibilities—wouldn't you be miffed if some new college grad were given the same entitlements within 6 months of arriving on the scene?

But there are more practical reasons, too. You can't start out on top, or even halfway up the ladder, until you learn the business.

*"Maybe so, Ken, but I already know how to pour coffee. I'm not learning anything."*

Well, not so fast.

I know entry level is frustrating. But while you're doing even these minor tasks, your bosses are watching to see if you're the kind of person who belongs in a higher position within the company. They're learning whether you're absorbing the company's culture (how to dress, how to conduct yourself professionally, how to leave the bulk of your personal life outside) and whether you have a knack for learning about what they do.

*"But making copies doesn't teach me about what they do."*

True, but handling responsibilities like this tells your boss that you're a team player and that you can do your appointed tasks efficiently and without any attitude. That's huge for them.

*"All right. I'll try to do these menial tasks without attitude. I'll sit in my cubicle all day long (or cashier's stool or wherever they want me to) and try not to get too distracted. But how do I fight off the gremlins? The voices that are now saying, 'You have to keep working here, whether you want to or not, to pay the bills.'"*

The way to keep your spirits up is to try to make your job, whatever it is, into something bigger.

Let's say that your job requires you to do A, B, and C: make copies, refill the coffee pot, and answer the phone. It's up to you to do these tasks well, but then also to figure out what D, E, and F are. What I'm talking about are *additional* things you can do that will further your personal interests, passion, and understanding of your workplace—and which might also (eventually) open up new doors. And to find these things you may have to look, as they say, outside the box.

❦

A story.

A friend of mine majored in art history, and what she really wanted to do was be an art dealer. But the entry-level job she found herself in soon after graduation was behind the cash register in a wine store!

So there she was, in entry-level hell, spending her days doing little more than ringing up bottles behind the register.

She felt completely depressed.

Enter the gremlins: *You're doing the wrong thing. . . . You're stuck here. . . . You'll be here forever. . . . Why did you even bother going to college at all?*

But my friend did her best to tune out the gremlins. She kept her head down, and by reading up on the different kinds of wine the store stocked, and by paying attention to what people bought and liked, she eventually became a wine advisor. She gained the trust of certain customers. They would actually call her before their dinner parties and say, "We're having pumpkin soup and rack of lamb—what kind of wine should we serve?" Her job was to match wines to the menu. She loved this new responsibility; it made her proud to be relied upon in this way, and yet she still wasn't doing what she wanted to do: deal in art.

Then, walking home from work one day, she had a lightbulb moment. She thought, *If these people trust me to choose wine for their dinner parties, maybe they'll trust me to choose art for their walls.*

Could it be true?

She decided to test the idea. She bought some modestly priced art and invited her wine clients to come see it.

Where? In her apartment!

And guess what? They bought it!

Next time around, she was able to spend a bit more money on the art, and by her third "showing," she was able to quit her job at the wine shop and rent a bona fide gallery space.

And before long, her gallery became very successful.

In other words, by thinking creatively about her situation and being open to experimentation when inspiration struck, she did it. She Six-Degreed her way to her dream career.

It took time, self-motivation, and a bit of financial risk—but it worked.

☙

*How did she do it?*

Well, as I said, my friend's first job, even though she had a college degree, was behind a cash register. She didn't dream that becoming an art dealer could possibly be connected to that job. Instead, she just felt like a low-paid clerk.

But let's look at this in terms of what we've discussed so far. How are these two jobs related—selling wine and dealing in art? What skill sets do they have in common? *How did she Six-Degree herself from one to the other?*

There are at least three categories: aesthetic skills, research skills, and sales skills.

Let's look for the connections.

First, aesthetic skills. In the wine field, she was using her nose and sense of taste (her mouth) to tell good wine from bad wine. In art, she used her eyes to tell good art from bad art.

Not exactly the same skill, but related.

Let's keep looking.

Second, research skills. In the wine shop, my friend had to access information on every vineyard and vintage. She needed to know, for example, that 2005 was a good year for Burgundy in France, and 2001 for Barolo in Italy. As an art dealer, she had to research a painting's history to provide its provenance (its ownership history) prior to sale—to be able to tell a prospective buyer, "In 2008, this painting sold from Gallery X in Paris to Mr. Y in Minneapolis," and so on.

Again, similar skills. But let's keep looking, because this is where it gets interesting.

Besides aesthetics and research, there's a sales skill required for each job, because (needless to say) if you don't sell wine, your wine store will close very fast—and if you don't sell art, you won't be an art dealer for long.

My friend insists she learned most of what she needed to know about art sales *behind the cash register in the wine store!*

In fact, she says:

*Her entry-level job as an art dealer took place in the wine store!*

And whether you're working in a wine store, in a coffee shop, behind the front desk in a dentist's office, or in a cubicle entering data until your eyes glaze over, the same can be true for you: You are probably learning essential skills that will help you transform your career down the line. You just have to put the time in now and trust that it will eventually lead to something new.

☙

*"Okay, I hear you. But it's so frustrating. How can I trust that these completely boring activities will lead me to something better down the line?"*

That's a big question.

Let's analyze it a bit more.

Tell me: What do you require in order to feel passion? Isn't that the goal? I'll say it another way: What does it take for you to be truly happy at work?

We all tend to come up with abstract answers. *"I need to like it." "I need to have fun."*

But instead of these kinds of answers, I'd like to think in terms of Six Degrees and skill sets.

Let's say, for our analysis, that to be truly happy at work, ideally my friend would have needed to exercise three skills she loved using: her aesthetic skill, her research skill, and her sales skill. For her, hitting all three of those notes, like playing three notes to make a chord on a piano, is what it would take for her to want to get out of bed in the morning and whistle her way to work. (She really does whistle, by the way.)

But how many skills did she use behind the cash register when she first started? For the most part, she was using only one: the sales skill—she was selling wine. So in the beginning, she wasn't playing a chord, but rather just one note, over and over and over, like a disturbing moment in a Stanley Kubrick movie. People came in and asked for a bottle of wine, she got it for them, and she rang it up. This, to her mind, made her no different from a cashier in a supermarket—in this case, a cashier with an art history degree.

And this is exactly why entry-level work is so frustrating.

When you're in your job in your cubicle, in the mailroom, or wherever you are, you would really want to play all of your notes, all of your skill sets. That's what it would take for you to roll over in bed in the morning and think, *This is going to be a great day.* That's what it would take to be happy. But in an entry-level position, you're probably using only one skill, if any. Using one skill represents forward progress, *even if it doesn't seem that way.* When your enjoyable skills are underemployed, it's natural to feel frustrated and depressed. Enter the gremlins, who say, "You're wasting your time here. Run!"

So what do you do?

How did my friend make it work for her?

She put herself out there. She attended all of the store's wine tastings (which tapped into her aesthetic interests) and studied the catalog whenever possible (tapping into her research interests), and if a customer came in for a mere bottle of table wine, she'd strike up a friendly conversation, learning everything she could about individual tastes (not to mention sales psychology) in the process.

Again, she wasn't consciously saying to herself, *I have these skill sets I need to use*. No, she didn't label things that way. She was just taking readily available steps to broaden the scope of her job.

⟊

How can you do it for yourself?

Let's say you're in the office. Maybe you could learn more about another department within the company and get to know the people who work in it?

What about doing some independent research on the firm's clients and accounts?

Or maybe you could offer to do some extracurricular research into new software, customers, advertising strategies, competitors, information technology, or some other aspect of the company that interests you. Then you could prepare a report on your findings and deliver it to your boss.

It may sound like I'm saying, "Find a mountain and climb it," when it's hard enough just dragging yourself to work each day. Yet this is one of the secrets of working yourself out of a frustrating entry-level situation: finding ways to make it more interesting. Keep reminding yourself that you're planting seeds of the job, or career area, you'll move to next.

Certainly it would be easier if someone would just tell you what to do, but often no one does. It's up to each one of us to figure it out for ourselves. The good news is that the different areas you try to explore—even if your efforts seem small and meaningless at the time—can lead to much bigger things later on.

For example, let's say you're the receptionist in a company with a marketing department, and marketing intrigues you. *I'm interested in that,* you might think. Or *It sounds better than what I'm doing now.*

During your lunch break, go to that department, introduce yourself to one of the people there, and politely ask for just a couple of minutes to discuss what it is that she does. If you're in a smaller company, you may already know the person, and you could engage her in a conversation more casually, maybe even over coffee or, if appropriate, over an after-work drink. Then make a point of checking in every couple of weeks to ask about new developments and to express your interest in any new opportunities. So long as you're very polite and respectful of your colleague's time, she should be receptive.

That's one step.

Does it sound easy? No, it's not. Because when you get back to your desk after lunch, or after the coffee date, you may feel like it was a totally worthless exercise. *What did I do? We just chatted for a few minutes. How's that possibly going to lead to anything new?*

But here's where the faith comes in: By pushing yourself to learn about and explore new areas, you'll eventually break out of where you are. It may not feel right while you're doing it. Just as if you were planting a seed in a garden, you don't have to feel happy that day for your activity to be successful—you just have to do it. With patience, the plants will come up from the seeds. And with patience, you'll reap real results.

Stepping out of your routine is the way to make things happen. Making entry level bearable and maybe even highly valuable requires you to put yourself out there, as we discussed in Chapter 3. Try to make this part of your lifestyle as much as you possibly can: to make new connections and pursue new activities. You're preparing yourself for what's going to come next.

∞

And if you run up against brick wall after brick wall . . . if absolutely no one at the office is receptive to your ideas and your eyes really do start to glaze over and you feel helpless to enhance the nature of your job in any meaningful way—and yet, for financial or ambition-related reasons, you just can't leave—then you'll have to consider some creative ways of pursuing your passions "around the edges," by which I mean outside of work. It's easy to get into a rut of waking up, going to work, staring at a computer all day, going home, eating dinner, and falling into bed. But if you can carve out an hour here and there—in the mornings, evenings, or weekends, or even during the occasional lunch break—and dedicate this precious personal time to activities that inspire and refresh you and maybe even get your mind working in the direction of a new career, the 9-to-5 grind will be much easier to bear.

Remember: *You won't be stuck in entry level forever.*

Although you're probably being squeezed into one skill area, you're learning more than you might think—and this is gradually but surely propelling you forward. It may seem slow and frustrating now, but you really are picking up information that may be useful down the road in ways you can't yet imagine. If you're in an office, for example, you're undoubtedly learning something subtle every single day: about organizational politics, about how to write professional and effective correspondence, about how to work as part of a team. You're also learning extremely valuable things about yourself, like whether you enjoy working with other people or independently, whether you do better work in the morning or afternoon, whether you prefer dealing with numbers or words, and so on.

Ultimately, no matter what kind of job you have, you'll leave the entry-level phase of life, one way or another. You'll get promoted or fired, or you'll choose to go.

People often wonder, *When should I leave?* I address this in the Frequently Asked Questions on page 109.

For now, keep in mind that the trick is to make it as interesting and advantageous as possible while you're there. Eventually your experience in the first job will lead you to the next thing— and one step closer to your ideal situation.

CHAPTER 8

## "I'M JUST IN IT FOR THE MONEY" AND DEFINITIONS OF SUCCESS

*If we'd known we were going to be the Beatles, we'd have tried harder.*

— GEORGE HARRISON

LOTS OF PEOPLE APPROACH THEIR career years thinking, *I just want to make money.*

Money's a good thing. It can help you live the good life, not to mention pay off school loans. But there's not a lot of good advice out there on how to go about making it. So, if you want to make big bucks, plain and simple, where can you turn?

Let's start with my imaginary friend Bill Gates.

"Hi, Bill."

"Hi, Ken."

"How are the wife and kids?"

"They're well, thanks."

"So, tell us, Bill: How did you make so much money?"

"Well, I went to Harvard, dropped out, and then I set about writing programs for a computer industry that didn't yet exist. For the first 10 years, what I was doing was worth about $2 an hour. Then I started Micro-soft and moved to

Seattle, we lost the hyphen (to become Microsoft), and I changed the world."

"Thank you, Bill."

Gulp.

Ummm. How do you follow in such footsteps? Do you start with getting into Harvard . . . just to drop out? And where would you find an enormous industry that doesn't exist yet?

Forget Bill. Let's try someone else.

Warren Buffett.

"How'd you do it, Warren?"

"Easy, Ken. I became the most gifted investor in the world."

"Thanks, Warren."

"No problem, Ken."

Hmmm. Are you supposed to put that on your Life After College "To Do" List? (1) Pick up the laundry. (2) Shop for dinner. (3) Become the most gifted investor in the world.

No. Let's forget Warren, too.

Here's the point: When people want to make money, they usually approach it in reverse. They look at people who've already made a fortune and try to emulate them. By extension, they look for specific "money areas"—jobs or industries in which making money seems to be a guaranteed outcome. Generally speaking, the big "money areas," which seem to promise big payoffs, are:

- Finance
- Information technology
- Media stardom
- Real estate

And for some people, in some parts of the country, law and medicine can be extremely profitable fields, as well. But here's the catch: Just because these are, for many people, "money areas," that doesn't mean they're necessarily money areas for you—and we're talking about you!

⟨☉⟩

No one can tell you exactly how to make money, but I can tell you how you probably won't: by making "money" your motivation without taking into account who you really are.

Think of it this way: Most people who are going to make money in, say, finance are going to be competing every day with colleagues who love finance and are talented in the field. Let's say Heather finds it boring, hates balancing her checkbook, and prefers to spend her time thinking about *anything else*. In that case, if she somehow lands a job in finance, she can't expect success to come easily or to enjoy herself along the way.

A guy once raised his hand during the Q&A at the end of one of my talks. He said that he planned to be an engineer, though he didn't want to be one. He said, "I'll be miserable, that's fine, but at least I'll succeed." I said, "You'll be miserable, yes, but you can't take it for granted that you'll succeed."

The bottom line: If you don't at least like what you do, you might succeed up to a point—and yes, you may sometimes take a job for a limited period of time strictly to gain a little financial security. But if those fields don't tap into any of your natural interests, you run the risk of burning out and feeling miserable, maybe even before the anticipated payoff comes through.

The truth is, successful people usually like what they're

doing—maybe not in entry-level positions, but in general. For example, when you're in the right field *for you,* you won't mind putting in extra time to get a project just right—and putting in that extra time separates you from those who *don't* get the promotions and big bonuses.

I'm always struck by how many people who have made billions have said that they weren't even thinking primarily about the money, but were focused on what they were doing.

Like Oprah. She says she never thought about money, just about her passion.

And Larry Page and Sergey Brin of Google. They stayed with it because *they loved what they were doing.*

This may sound like obvious advice—try to do something you'll enjoy—but, well . . . you'd be surprised.

I'm sure many of you have been told, "You can do anything." And it's true. This is America. There are limitless possibilities. You can do anything, or at least give it a shot, and if you work hard, there's a chance you'll do reasonably well.

And yet, the most successful people do better than "reasonably well." Perhaps it's true, we can do anything and no one else can stop us on our career paths, but at some point we stop ourselves when we're not *into it.* You'll have a better chance to go all the way if you're fully engaged with your heart, as well as your mind.

That's the ideal.

Now, as we've discussed, you may have to get started by doing just anything to get by financially while also taking steps to figure out the bigger picture. When you put yourself out there and get your first job, you may find yourself in the wrong area, or in one that would work better for someone else—your best friend, maybe, or your brother. As I've already said: That's okay. It happens all the time. We've discussed how all roads lead to Rome, which means that your efforts in one area can accelerate your success in one you enjoy more.

But as a general rule, I'd ask you to do one thing. *Attempt, if possible, to keep thinking of what your passions are as you go* (see Chapter 6) *and try to always get closer to an area that feels right—one that taps into one or more of those passions.*

❦

So this brings us back to the question, what's the best path for you?

Let's say you were thinking of medical school, but you really wanted to be something else.

Story time.

Once upon a time, there was a premed student who dropped out of school to follow his passion, which was to become a track coach.

He succeeded. He was a great success in his job at the University of Oregon, coaching his team to four NCAA titles.

And then one day he noticed how absurdly heavy his team's running shoes were. (As they all were at the time—it was the Jurassic era of athletic footwear.)

So what did he do? He went home and poured rubber onto his waffle iron. And out of the waffle iron he pulled the prototype for the first lightweight, waffle-soled shoe—at which point a lightbulb came on.

He and one of his runners put up $500 each to launch the brand. They named their company after the winged Greek goddess of victory.

Yes, Nike.

Philip Knight, billionaire and CEO, was the runner. Bill Bowerman, the other billionaire, was the coach.

They founded what would become one of the most recognizable, lucrative brands in the world, and all by simply doing what they loved.

America is arguably the best place in the world in which to make a run of it as an entrepreneur, as these two did (literally). And this is true even in tough economic times, when one hears about people who've been laid off but view their "bad luck" as an opportunity to do something they always wanted to do—like start up their own Web site design company or launch a new series of travel guides. Think of Blake Mycoskie, founder of TOMS Shoes, which designs and sells lightweight shoes based on an Argentinian design—and for each pair sold gives one to a child in need. Like Knight and Bowerman, he started with no more in his bank account than your average college grad has. All of these entrepreneurs just set their minds to doing something new—or something old, but in a new or more efficient way—and executed it very well.

And doing something very well is a lot easier if you enjoy doing it.

Now, some of you may be thinking, *But I'm not an entrepreneur. I'd like to prove myself in a bigger arena.*

Read on.


## WHAT ABOUT THE CORPORATE TRACK?

What about working for a consulting firm, an investment bank, a movie studio, an ad agency, the world's largest producer of breakfast cereal or bottled iced tea, a network, or an airplane manufacturer?

For some of you, the idea of working for a large corporation may not be as sexy as striking out on your own. It goes against our American ideal of the self-made entrepreneur. Why do you think so many politicians like to be photographed by the ocean or clearing brush? Because being a rugged loner "on his own" is as American as apple pie. If they're photographed hobnobbing with rich corporate types, they're going to look like, well, rich corporate types—a category of Americans who, these days at least, endure a lot of suspicion.

But there is no getting around the fact that the global economy is a vast network of corporations, and working for one such corporation could potentially prove very lucrative and exciting for you. People make fortunes.

So, how do you know if you're a good fit for the corporate world?

Let's see. For the most part, you'd have to be comfortable wearing a suit a lot of the time. And sitting at a desk, behind a computer, 5 days a week, at least in the beginning.

You'd have to be mature, polished, strategic, sometimes competitive, not afraid of working long hours, a team player, comfortable, patient with and even excited about testing yourself within a hierarchical structure (with someone above you and someone below), willing to travel a lot, confident enough to make presentations and lead meetings, or at least willing to learn how to do so, and reasonably able to manage stress.

Does this sound like you? If you've always dreamed of working your way up in a big company and maybe even eventually traveling to many different places to meet with clients and devise new strategies, then I say, go for it!

And remember, when the cameras stop clicking, brush-clearing and ocean-lounging presidents usually get back into their high-tech helicopters to go home.

There's lots of money to be made in the corporate world, *if it's the right place for you.*

## WILL I MAKE *ANY* MONEY AT *THIS* JOB?

What about the arts, or teaching, or another area that doesn't seem to pay well?

The truth is, sometimes we don't choose our professions—they choose us.

If there's no question in your mind that you want to be a doctor or a physicist, you'll follow a very prescribed academic course, and you'll probably be paid consistently and reasonably well. But what if you're drawn to a different kind of "passion area," one that traditionally doesn't pay well, except to those at the very top?

Let's take the arts first.

There's a story about someone who asked if he should be an actor. The answer was "If you have to ask the question, then no."

I think this is a pretty good rule for all the arts.

Achieving success as a professional actor or creative artist of any kind—a writer, painter, musician, photographer—is incredibly hard. When you're starting out, the nature of the business involves intense and repeated rejection, which can be difficult to take. And the odds of actually earning a reasonable salary are quite small, considering the ratio of how many people attempt it to how many actually "make it"—or even get paid at all.

If you're wondering whether or not you should go for it, I'd say this: If your passion for your creative pursuit is so great that you would be *miserable* if it weren't the focus of your life, then of course, go for it. In fact, you don't need me to tell you that. You're going to do it no matter what I tell you.

On the other hand, if you *don't* feel an intense need to do it and you go for it anyway, the day will come when you'll need to find extra strength and perseverance—that's if success doesn't come quickly and easily, of course. Naturally, those who "go for it" in the arts are not risk averse. They're more than okay with a certain amount of instability.

If you do decide to pursue a career in the arts, here's some advice: Get as much training as possible, expose yourself to as much of the medium as possible, and *learn how to take criticism.* If you don't have a thick skin, you'll need to grow one. You can start to do this by truly listening to and considering other people's reactions to your work. When we ask for feedback, usually we're hoping to hear that what we've done is fantastic. But that's rarely what we're told, nor how we learn. True artists come to understand that they learn and grow *the most* when people don't simply tell them what they want to hear. If you're good, you'll eventually develop a sixth sense for discerning what feedback is important and relevant and what isn't—when people are wasting your time and when they're telling you what you need to know.

And as for the financial prospects?

We'll get there.

But first, a word about teaching, and other seemingly non-lucrative passions.

In my mind, the word *teacher* is inextricably linked with the words *noble profession*. (Try it. Say "teacher" if you ever meet me, and I'll say "noble profession.") Teaching is such hard work, and the stakes are so high, I'm blown away by teachers who manage to show up and be that critical inspiration day after day, year after year, and—in some cases—decade after decade. What a talent!

I recently met a group of elementary school teachers nearing retirement. They were all still just as passionate about teaching as they were when they started. Were any of them rich? I think it's safe to say no, they weren't. But they all told me that they wouldn't have traded their professional lives for any other.

Why?

Because if you're truly passionate about something, then *doing it will be its own reward*. For teachers who love teaching, and painters who love painting, and writers who love writing, and pianists who love playing the piano—teaching/painting/ writing/playing the piano is an end in itself.

And I can think of other areas to which this applies, as well. Maybe you're passionate about tennis, and you want to build your career around that, but you aren't exactly Roger Federer or one of the Williams sisters. You're pretty certain that tennis, for you, isn't the fast track to making millions, but you *love* tennis, you could play it all day every day and never lose interest, and it makes you feel happy and healthy and strong. So why not become a coach, or a counselor at a tennis camp, or an employee at a tennis equipment shop, and see where that takes you? Your passion may just propel you toward some unimaginable success, like someday owning a beautiful tennis complex or being *director* of the tennis camp, either of which can provide a decent living or even a lucrative one.

Most important, though: You will have spent years doing what you love. As long as you can figure out a way to make *enough* money for the basics and to support a family (should you choose to have one), any additional money you make as a result of following your passion will be icing on the cake.

Maybe you won't feel fulfilled all the time, but you'll feel that way a lot of the time, so that one day you can look back on your life and say to yourself, "I made the most of it. I lived well."

☙

Money goes a long way toward helping you live well, to be sure. And in this country, if you do what you love in a way that gives something valuable to other people, you have a good chance of making a lot of money. Yet there are other aspects of success that are equally important and reliable: staying true to yourself, having a positive influence on the lives of others, and negotiating a life that reflects what you feel you're here to do.

A lot of people will offer you their advice on the topic of money—how to earn it, what to do with it, where to get more of it. Especially in a bad economy, making money may seem to be a high priority. And to an extent, it should be. But your particular answer to the money question will depend on you: who you are, what you're best suited to do, and what you think you may enjoy doing.

CHAPTER 9

# FREQUENTLY ASKED
# QUESTIONS ABOUT CAREERS

**Q:** *How do I interpret people not responding to my job
applications? Should I assume I approached them in the
wrong way? Or is there something wrong with my
résumé?*

**A:** What you can probably assume is that the person who
received your résumé received a whole pile of résumés.
There could be hundreds of applicants for any given
position. It's a numbers game, so it's not really a personal
rejection. But you should always do everything you can to
make sure your résumé is as professional as it can be.

What does that mean?

Résumés should be clear, concise, consistently formatted,
and *proofread*. Many employers will simply throw out a résumé
or cover letter that contains a typo or misspelling. So it's worth
it to spend a good deal of time working on your résumé, consulting sample formats online for guidance, and then having
someone else look it over—maybe even hiring a professional editor to ensure that you've presented yourself in the best and most
professional light. There are ways to make narrow or limited job

experience really shine on the page, but sometimes it takes a second pair of eyes. So don't hesitate to ask for help. It can make a big difference.

While we're on the subject, cover letters are also extremely important. Unless you've been explicitly instructed otherwise, you should never send just a résumé alone. Most likely, it'll get deleted or tossed. Your cover letter is your opportunity to say something personal and memorable about yourself and to make a case for your suitability for the job in question. It should also be well written, free of typos and grammatical errors, and respectful—by which I mean (1) you should spell the name of its recipient correctly—*this is very important!*—and (2) you shouldn't ramble on for too long. In most cases, one page or less is ideal.

One more note on the topic of how you present yourself to a prospective employer. Once you have applied for a job, the person reading your application has, at her fingertips, an instantaneous way of learning more about you: the Internet. She might very well Google you if she likes your résumé. What she finds will amount to, basically, an extension of your application. So before you apply for any jobs, Google *yourself* to see how you might come across. Are there any compromising photos from spring break? Embarrassing blog posts or unprofessional Facebook updates? Now is your chance to delete them or to exercise a Web site's privacy options, if possible. If you can't wipe clean your virtual slate, at least prepare yourself to answer any questions it raises down the line.

If you've done this, and you've created a polished, professional résumé and cover letter, the rest is out of your control. (See also Chapter 23.)

Q: *Is it true that when it comes to finding a job, it's not what you know, but who you know?*

A: Yes, it's true—that is a big part of it. Many things in your life will depend on who you know, from getting a doctor's referral to meeting your future spouse. Knowing someone, or having an "in," is often how people get hired. The good news is this: If you don't have those contacts, you can make them, especially at the entry level. That's the meaning of "putting yourself out there" (see Chapter 3). That's the reason to set up a few informational interviews. Every time you meet someone new, your web of contacts grows. If you're a little shy about meeting people, this is the time to start getting out there—because every time you do, you're building the skills to do it more effectively the next time.

Q: *How do I know when to leave a job—especially an entry-level position?*

A: In large part, this has to be a personal judgment call. A lot of people just reach a point where they know they can't face their job or boss or office for one more day, so they find another source of income and make the leap. But before you do anything drastic, consider this: You might think you hate your job, but is it really the job you hate— or is it the sometimes exhausting intensity of the 9-to-5 life? In school, maybe you were able to schedule your courses so you didn't have to get up too early. After that easy schedule, early morning work of any kind is going to be a shock. And in school, you could walk outside between classes, see the sun, chat with friends. Now, you may not even be able to make personal calls during the day. The workday, to the uninitiated, can feel a little like life in prison—especially if you're not doing work that interests you. The progression from school—which may have seemed like "the good life"—to entry level, which can feel like mindless, humiliating labor—is often painful. But you will, eventually, get over that hump and find your way into a position that makes you feel happier and more fulfilled. The trick is not to sabotage yourself by getting discouraged too early.

Let's take an example. Say you want to work in television, and you've landed a job at CBS. You've been fetching coffee, making photocopies, and answering phones for 6 months now. You feel like it's getting harder and harder to justify the fortune spent on your education when your hourly wage after taxes is in the area of $12.

But here's the thing: The television industry is corporate. And in corporations, you're not going to come in at a high level when you're 22 or even 25 years old. Your immediate challenge is simply to get in—which you've already done. The next challenge is to excel at what you might consider to be meaningless work, and to climb your way up the ladder, rung by rung.

The fact is, only half of corporate CEOs went to business school. The other half were liberal arts majors. And here's another piece of good news: Only 30 percent of those CEOs went to Ivy League schools.

In other words, getting in on the ground floor is *the* route to moving up. It's the way in—even if it does involve seemingly menial tasks and minimal pay, for now.

So if you're already working within the industry you want to pursue, and if you've landed one of those prized entry-level jobs at a well-known company in your field, it's probably worth sticking with it for as long as you can—until you're promoted, you get another offer that really interests you, or you decide that you feel more passionate about pursuing something else and can make that happen. (See Chapter 7.)

Q: *I'm an entrepreneur. I've started my own tutoring company [or] I'm a freelance Web site designer. So far, I've been pretty successful working for myself. I'm wondering—should I go for it, or should I get a "regular" job?*

A: The laws in this country are designed for entrepreneurs, so if you're young and excited about your current work, why not go for it?

You do need to be comfortable with a certain level of risk. I've already mentioned how Bill Gates was paid the equivalent of $2 an hour for his first 10 years with Microsoft. Doing your own thing is not necessarily a path to job security. Many people who start their own companies fail. But entrepreneurship has made a great many fortunes, as well.

The way to go forward is to learn all you can about the field, make as many contacts as you can, and be active on all levels. As a businessman. An innovator. A marketer. You'll also have to structure your own days and solve the problem of health insurance, which most freelancers need to purchase for themselves. But if you enjoy what you're already doing, and you're making money, and you're realistic about the risks it involves, why not continue? One way to do it is to give yourself a fixed amount of time—say, 3 years. And if after 3 years you aren't happy with your progress and prospects, you can always shift to a more conservative path.

> Q: *I'm graduating soon, and I'm thinking of joining the Peace Corps, traveling, or living abroad for a while. I'm not sure what I want to do for a career, but I think I might enjoy doing PR for a restaurant. Which should I do? And will I lose time if I take a year off?*
>
> A: This is another decision that ultimately will require a personal judgment call, taking into account all the relevant factors. But I do have some advice to offer.

Programs like the Peace Corps not only do a lot of good in the world, but also give many people meaningful experiences that they cherish forever. And I have never met anyone for whom living abroad wasn't an enriching life experience. It broadens you as a person; it changes your perspective.

But let's face it: In some ways, you could also be very confused when you get back. Returning home from a foreign country always requires a big adjustment. And if you're ambivalent about what you want to do now, living in Tanzania won't necessarily make your choice any clearer.

But that's not necessarily a reason not to do it.

Another consideration is how the economy is affecting the restaurant industry right now. Are lots of restaurants thriving in your area? What are the implications of postponing your job plans for a year based on the current circumstances within the industry? But also weigh the fact that all of us start over in life from time to time. Will you be so far behind if you wait one extra year to get started? That's what you need to consider.

And finally, let's not forget the experience itself. You may discover what you really want to do in the time that you are away, and you may meet valuable contacts. Changing your surroundings, and your perspective, may change your definition of your "dream job."

Q: *What if I start in restaurant PR now and apply to go into the Peace Corps a year from now? If I go, will I lose the connections I've already made? Would it be crazy to go at that time?*

A: If you start working now, then you'll have a year to get experience in the field and get to know whether you like it and are on the right path. And if you realize you don't like it, you'll still have learned new things and refined your direction—which is no small feat.

In fact, if you really like the field, then after a year you may not want to leave. You need to keep your mind open to that possibility. On the other hand, after a year you may be *more* than ready to go. So you should probably apply for the Peace Corps now and decide later whether it's what you're actually going to do.

Will you lose your career connections if you go away? You might, to an extent. But that's not a reason not to go, if you really want to. You will still have made a good start in the field, and, provided you did your work with integrity, some of the people you encountered may be happy to reemploy you when you get back.

**Q:** *I have so many passions, I don't know where to begin. I want to be a journalist. Or maybe a therapist. And I'm thinking of joining the army! But I feel that if I follow one, I'll be giving up on the others.*

**A:** Wow! It's good to have choices. You're lucky. Having a lot of passions is a good thing.

This is not the kind of thing to lose sleep over. We've spoken about how you'll probably have more than one career. Do I mean you'll do all three of these? Possibly. Or you may end up in a career requiring skill sets that will satisfy the desires for these three.

How can you begin to decide among the current possibilities? Well, to take this specific example, therapists tend to work for themselves. But in the army you're part of a conservative organization with lots of structure and rules. And depending on which publications they work for, and in what capacity, journalists work within yet a different framework of structure and independence.

So you could begin by asking yourself, "How do I feel about structure versus independence?" This could help you narrow your choices quickly.

Or, if you choose to become a therapist but you're also a very patriotic person who might enjoy the culture and structure of the army, you could be a therapist for soldiers or veterans. You could serve this same function in some other service-related organization—say, working in a school—rather than in private practice.

And you could write articles about your experiences, as well, to satisfy your passion for journalism.

The point is this: Try to think of which career is a good starting point. This will involve both a rational analysis and an assessment of what opportunities are available.

And once you take steps in one direction, don't worry about the others. You're lucky to have identified just one passion, let alone three—and chances are that along the way, you'll be able to draw on skill sets that will satisfy you on more than one track. (See Chapter 2.)

Q: *What about grad school? Should I go?*

A: If you know for certain what you want to do, or if you have a very strong inclination toward a particular field, and if this career requires a master's degree or a PhD, then yes. You should go. The time and money you'll spend will be worth it.

But I suspect that, if you're asking the question, you're not certain about what you want to do, and you're considering grad school or law school just because it's something to do or you feel it might be worthwhile.

In which case I would say you should go only if you have some genuine interest in the field. Grad school takes some people more than 5 years to complete, and it costs a small fortune. So it may sound impressive to say, "I'm going to law school" or "I'm going to get a PhD in medieval history"—but if the subjects themselves aren't of interest to you, and if you don't have any desire to do something in these fields down the line—when you might be tens or hundreds of thousands of dollars in debt—you need to ask yourself whether grad school is just an end in itself. It may be your way of doing *something,* but not necessarily something that will make you happy careerwise in the long run.

Now, as I have said: All kinds of experiences teach us useful things and lead to other things, many of them better and more fulfilling. So going to grad school just because you don't know what else to do won't be a totally unrewarding choice. You'll meet new people and encounter new ideas, and perhaps even discover a new, more appealing direction while you're there. It's really just a question of whether the time you will spend, coupled with the tremendous financial outlay, will seem worth what you gained once you've graduated and start paying back your loans. It might be better to explore less expensive ways to learn more about yourself and what you'd like to do . . . maybe starting with Chapter 6.

> **Q:** *I studied to be a teacher. I want to get a master's, but I don't know if I should take an entry-level teaching job right away instead. I don't need the master's to get the job, but I will probably need one eventually to move up. What should I do?*
>
> **A:** In tough economic times, areas that used to be safe, like teaching, are more competitive. Why? People who have lost jobs in other areas may follow their long-lost dream of becoming a teacher.

Therefore, if you don't need the degree to get the job, I'd say just try to find a job, especially one you like. There's probably a way to get the degree along the way, at night or on weekends.

But I'd also say that you should send out applications to

master's programs now, so that if you don't find a job, you'll still have options.

Remember: Life doesn't always proceed in a straight line. But if you are thoughtful and keep your eyes open, things have a way of working out.

> Q: *You mentioned law school earlier, and . . . I'm really confused. I don't really want to go, but I feel like I'm headed that way anyway. Help!*
>
> A: What I said applies to grad school in general, but definitely to law school in particular. Imagine trying to build a pyramid. Hard work, right? I can't imagine how they did it. But going to law school is the modern version of building a pyramid. That's how hard it is.

Next, imagine building a pyramid with one hand tied behind your back. As if it weren't challenging enough, right? Yet if you're going to law school and you're not sure you want to be there, you'll be doing the work with only one hand.

But here's the thing: Couldn't it be said that the person who could build a pyramid with only one hand is even stronger than all the others? I think so.

You may be going to school for the right reasons or the wrong reasons. Yet once you decide to do it, it represents a kind of passion to accomplish such a huge task, even halfheartedly.

I know what you may be thinking. *Passion? Are you kidding? I'm* dreading *it!* To you it might not seem like an achievement, because you feel as if you're being dragged there kicking and screaming. But who's dragging you, really? *You* are—and this is a fact, even if you tell yourself, *Well, I'm doing it for my parents,* or *I'm going because I feel that I should.* It's still ultimately your choice and responsibility. So I'd repeat: This is, in fact, a variety of *passion.* Let's call it the kicking-and-screaming, I-don't-want-to-do-this-*but-I-will-anyway-because-something-about-it-seems-right* variety of passion.

So if you're saying, "I don't want to go to law school, but I feel I *should,*" or "I don't want to do this, but I feel myself headed that way anyway," and, at the same time, you can think of a good reason *not* to go, then don't go. Walk away. I'm not talking about just coming up with a rationalization or justification for doing nothing at all; I mean coming up with something else you'd rather do instead—and *will* do. In that case, you'll be saving yourself the money, and you'll be trying what you really want, rather than a career that might not be your first choice.

But if you can't think of a better thing to do, and you decide to go through with law school because it's the strongest magnet for you right now, don't be afraid. You may be doing it for perfectly valid reasons that you're not even aware of at the moment and won't be aware of for some time.

You might even like it more than you expect.

And what if law doesn't work out? If you took a survey of lawyers who don't practice anymore, you'd likely find some compelling answers.

I conducted my own informal survey among three friends who happen to be nonpracticing lawyers. One woman, Jen, a corporate lawyer who stopped practicing at 34 to raise a family, said she had no regrets.

"Law teaches you to think in a different way," she said, "so it's useful, even if you don't become a lawyer, or you don't continue practicing all your life. I was recently on a board with lawyers and nonlawyers. When we had to evaluate potential candidates for a job, the other lawyers and I were able to make fast decisions. We asked questions the others didn't and saw applicants in ways the others couldn't. . . . Being a lawyer was also good for my self-confidence when I was in my late twenties and early thirties."

Another friend, Liliana, is a very gifted and successful clothing designer in New York City. She said, "Having studied law prepared me to be successful in business. It was good training."

And my third former-lawyer friend, Bill, a man who retired at 40 after selling his business for somewhere in the mid–eight figures, said he wouldn't do law school again, but it absolutely helped him. I asked him what he could possibly mean by that. He said, "I hated every minute of law school and wouldn't want to live through it a second time. I only practiced law for a year—yet it was helpful. . . . If you have the right personality and you get a job with the right firm, you can make contacts with successful people and win their trust. These are possible lifelong connections or mentors. In business, without the law degree, say, if I were a low-level banking exec, I wouldn't have had such fast access to that caliber of people."

In the year he practiced, he befriended a client of the firm who became his mentor and who led him to a career in real estate. With that, he was on his way. Interestingly, however, his eventual business, which led to his great prosperity when he sold it, wasn't related to real estate.

He says he made the contacts for *that* business on the tennis court.

Because, as I said: One thing leads to another.

# PART 2

## RELATIONSHIPS

# CHAPTER 10

# SKETCHES

*Experience is a good teacher, but she sends in terrific bills.*

—MINNA ANTRIM

IF YOU JUST GRADUATED FROM college, you might not be looking for The One, but sooner or later you might. We'll get to that.

First, I'd like to discuss a situation that's pretty common in one's twenties: living in the world of the sketch.

It goes like this, in four easy steps.

1. **Meet** someone.

2. **Feel** a great connection.

3. **Think,** *Whoa. This is going to be important,* and then . . .

4. **It's over.**

Don't worry. This is normal. I'm not even necessarily talking about actual relationships, just false alarms. But relationships can go that way, too.

1. **Meet** someone.

2. **Feel** a great connection.

3. **Keep it going** over a series of days, weeks, or even months.

4. **Think,** *This is going to be important—maybe it's even The One,* and then . . .

5. **It's over.**

Any questions?

When I was in my twenties, I met a woman at an art opening in Manhattan one evening. She was smart and attractive. After some chatting, we left and took the subway together. I asked for her number, and she wrote it on my hand, while the subway swayed back and forth. This seemed to me the height of coolness.

After we went our separate ways, the whole rest of my way home, I stared at my hand. All she'd written was "K" and her number. Amazing!

When I got home, I wrote the number on a piece of paper, and a few days later, I called her. And for weeks, we played phone tag. We talked about getting together. I think we even made a plan, but then I had to go out of town for some reason, or she got sick, or . . . I can't remember. The point is this: We never saw each other again.

The End.

That's my story.

Did you like it?

No, nothing ever happened.

Why? I can't be certain, but I think it had to do with this: While I was copying this girl's phone number down that first night, I was thinking about how she and I had held our glasses of white wine in the gallery and looked at the art together and it was really great. And then I thought about how, later, swaying in the subway car, she had done this writing-on-my-hand thing, and that was great, too. But I also remembered that she had spoken a lot about her family. And she had said it was great that my name was Ken, because she and everyone in her family had names that began with a *K*.

And something about this little detail slowed me down.

This woman seemed to be thinking about how I might fit into her family already, the very first night we met.

If it were me *now*, and I were single, I'd be flattered. And thrilled.

But me *then?* No way.

She hadn't come off as desperate, by any means. I still thought she was elegant and confident and, as I've said, cool. And yet still, because of where *I* was in life, her references to her family made me uncomfortable, because I wasn't ready to have a committed relationship.

I guess what I wanted instead was to be the kind of guy a girl might look at and say, "Maybe I'll try this guy out, but no way would I marry him! Not in a million years!"

And yet, it was even more complicated than that. Even if I wasn't ready to be in a committed relationship, I could still put a ladder up on my roof and see KEN = COMMITTED off in the distance. Not too far off.

So why was I so reluctant *then?*

She was fantastic, beautiful, a keeper.

So what was wrong with me? A mystery. I spent weeks asking myself questions.

"Did I do something wrong?"

"Did I say something wrong?"

### INSTRUCTIONS SHOULD YOU FIND YOURSELF
### IN A SIMILAR CIRCUMSTANCE

1. Continue asking the preceding five-word unanswerable questions until physically exhausted.

2. If bored, substitute "Is something wrong with me?" for variety's sake.

3. Fall asleep, wake up the next day, and continue.

4. Repeat until you achieve your goal: making yourself thoroughly miserable over an extended period of time.

In my case, this was a few weeks.

But I shouldn't have beaten myself up about it so much.

It was just a sketch.

I just wasn't ready.

Now, to clarify: I am *not* saying it's okay to treat people in a totally disrespectful way. If you meet a cool guy in Starbucks and you start talking and make a plan to have coffee again the following week, I'm not saying you should just blow it off—so don't fail to show up, and don't send him a text 5 minutes before you're supposed to be there to cancel. Sketches that go nowhere because you aren't ready are okay. Sketches that go nowhere because you're an inconsiderate jerk are another story.

But provided everyone behaves well enough, not feeling ready for a serious relationship—and, more important, *knowing* that you aren't ready—can be a good thing. It just means that you need more time to sort out some issues of your own—issues that, until you've lived with them a little bit longer and can recognize them and learn how to manage them, will work against you.

How?

They'll get in the way of a long-term relationship with someone else.

For example, in my case, I used to worry whether being committed to someone would feel like being in prison.

But eventually I was able to tell myself, *No, Ken. It won't.*

I also used to wonder, *Will this relationship smother me?*

But eventually I got to *Shut up, Ken. It won't.*

We'll talk about these kinds of inner roadblocks a bit more later. I can't tell you exactly what happened to help me get over them, to evolve from *Will this relationship kill all my freedom and autonomy?* to the much more mature and productive *Shut up, Ken. It won't.* It was a gradual process having to do with the accumulation of experiences and ideas and the passage of time.

As it will be for you, too.

It's bound to happen: A new person will appear, the situation will seem loaded with promise, but then, for reasons confusing even to you, you won't feel comfortable taking it further.

And it will end there.

Or maybe you'll keep going, and it won't be a long-term relationship, but you'll still learn some things; you'll pick up one or more of the many small or even large lessons about getting along. And this will begin to prepare you for the relationships that will come later.

So, it's all good, as long as you handle it as well as you can at the end and are forgiving of yourself.

So what are sketches?

Often, they're just perky signs that say **NOT READY!** or **SORT OF READY, BUT PROCEED WITH CAUTION.**

**Sometimes they just pique our interest.** Check out all the listings people post under "missed connections" online. Like, "I saw you in the park. You were wearing a green jacket. We smiled." Or "You: brown eyes, brown leather jacket. You winked at me (or maybe you had something in your eye?)." But I tend to think that when it's right, you don't miss the connection. You walk right up, say something stupid about her jacket, she says thank you or "You're a jerk, go away," and either way you know where you stand.

**Sometimes they hurt.** Say a new couple connects, and they start hanging out, and the guy falls really hard for the girl—and then, 3 weeks later, she tells him that her boyfriend of 4 years is on his way back from a hiking trip in the Rockies.

In this case, it can be messy. Relationships are messy. But if we can understand that we're always learning—about ourselves and our ability to relate—we can take comfort in the idea that we're always moving toward something better with the person coming to us next.

So how do you know which sketches are going to evolve into something serious and which aren't?

You don't need to know.

In fact, sometimes things go better when you don't.

When I met my wife, Bette, many years after K-girl, I wasn't thinking, *Whoa! This is the big one!* and neither was Bette. And yet it *was* the big one—probably because neither of us was obsessed with "Is she or isn't she?" or "Is he or isn't he?" when we first met. We just had a good time.

And I was only able to keep things going with Bette, and eventually feel that I could commit to her, because of all the sketches and also some longer-term connections that had come before. And by the way: A couple of those longer relationships *did* make me feel like I was in prison, and ended painfully, but it's thanks to those that I was able to get closer to the real thing.

And you know what?

It was worth it.

That's why I think it isn't right to say that early attempts at relationships are a waste of time. Don't beat yourself up with questions like "Why was I ever with *him?*" or "How could I have wasted so much time with *her?*" Those experiences are exactly what prepare us for the good things to come.

We'll talk about this more in later chapters.

Meanwhile, if you feel eager for something significant to happen in your love life, but you also feel frustrated because you're forever in the world of the sketch, take the hint. You may just not be ready. For some people, it's years before they're able to be in a committed relationship with confidence and ease. And that's fine.

That's not to say that people don't get swept off their feet and it doesn't lead to love. I think that happens every day. But in my case, all those false starts and relationships that didn't make it—which are nice to remember now but were excruciating at the time—well, they just *couldn't* have worked out. It wasn't time.

So what about you? How do you deal in the meantime? Should you be celibate? Should you not? Should you avoid going out altogether?

Everyone's needs are different, but I think that some of the advice in the following pages will help you address your own needs.

For now, the message is just this: If you're looking for The One and not finding him or her, you don't have to wallow in despair, but you can get busy.

How?

By preparing yourself in inner and outer ways, so you'll be ready when someone who *is* right for you arrives.

# CHAPTER 11

# ON YOUR OWN

Need coauthor for book on self-reliance.

—ANONYMOUS NEWSPAPER AD

ONE OF THE BEST WAYS to prepare for a serious relationship is to learn how to be okay on your own.

It sounds counterintuitive, doesn't it? Like saying the best way to find a partner is to move to a desert island.

But it's true.

First, a few disclaimers:

Relationships come on their own schedules. That's not to say that you shouldn't put yourself out there and keep your eyes open, but you can't force them.

Maybe you've been asked to be the best man at your buddy's wedding, or maybe your best friend just got engaged. And some of your other friends are already married. So you're going to be a best man or a bridesmaid *again*. And you're wondering, *What's wrong with me? Shouldn't I be next, and soon?*

It's important to remember that these things happen, or don't happen, for lots of reasons—many of them beyond your control. There's no reason to pressure yourself to be in a serious relationship if you're not in one. Not to mention that these days, approximately half of all marriages end in divorce. Choosing too quickly or under pressure could be your fast track to joining the club.

Now, sometimes people need a little outside pressure to take a long-term relationship to the next level. And who are we kidding—sometimes the pressure's there anyway, and we have to deal with it.

*"Mom, please."*

*"Honey, really."*

If someone is pressuring you, well, the trick is to find as much personal space as possible. A choice made under too much pressure probably won't lead to a connection strong enough to last.

Remember: Someone great for you is out there—probably even lots of people—but one of them will only come along at the right time. The right time for you, *and* the right time for him or her.

So . . . relax.

You can't force it. Now, here's another thing to consider:

Not everyone needs to be in a relationship.

Some people are fine on their own.

Some people won't *ever* want to get married. Which is okay.

And while we're at it, some people may not want to have kids. That's okay, too.

But say you *do* want to be with someone, and you're really impatient, feeling like you're not getting anywhere. How do you deal with being alone? How do you get ready?

By living your life.

Preparing *yourself.*

Sounds like we're back to the desert island, so let's break it down.

What are we really looking for when we say we're looking for someone long-term?

Sex?

Yes, good sex is important, but it's no guarantee that you'll stay together. And what happens when you aren't in bed?

Companionship?

Also important.

But I'd put it this way: We're looking for someone we're attracted to, whom we respect, and with whom we can imagine ourselves navigating life well. An ally, a friend, and someone sexy, all rolled into one. Someone to love us and be loved by us. Someone with whom, ideally, we would each be the best person we could be, and also someone with whom we would have a great time.

What's the best way to find such a person?

The comedian Jonathan Winters once said, "I couldn't wait for success, so I went ahead without it."

In this case, I'd say you should tell yourself, "I can't wait for my relationship to show up, so I'm going to get started without it."

Sounds good. But how?

Consider this: Sometimes people who are desperate for a relationship spend their time "waiting" for it, rather than living.

It's a passive way to be, and you end up spending your time worrying about why your life isn't how you want it to be.

But that kind of thinking doesn't tend to result in making your life the way you want it to be.

Think about it: If you're hoping that someone wonderful will just show up and then you'll be happy, rather than discovering ways of making *yourself* happy, it's kind of like saying, "What's my partner going to give me?"

And this "What's in it for me?" attitude is a stone's throw from "A partner will solve all my problems."

And this logic, in turn, is only inches away from a childlike assumption that "Mom or Dad will solve my problems."

Gulp.

The thing is, being this way doesn't draw people to us. As Marianne Williamson once said, "No guy says to his friend, 'I met this fabulous desperate woman at a party last night.'"

Or vice versa, with women and desperate guys. I talked earlier in the book about volunteering. It applies here, too. Consider this: When people volunteer, they get back as much as or even more than they give. And this *actively* teaches them the law by which intimate relationships work.

It's a key lesson. By extending yourself to others, you demonstrate that you know that giving leads to receiving. Not in some kind of exact equation, "I give this so now I'll get that" way, but in more subtle and even magical ways.

The point is, giving is the initiating force.

Besides volunteering, there are other ways you can practice giving—by giving to yourself and learning to enjoy your life. Enjoying a sports event, a concert, an exhibit, or just some dinner with friends.

It's important to remember that your eventual partner won't be able to save you steps. So it's a good idea to take your time in No-Boyfriend Land or No-Girlfriend Land and use it to do the work of becoming the person you want to be, the best version of you.

Think about it this way: The goal is to be a person *you* would want to know, a person *you* would want to be with, a person *you* would like to find sitting across the table from *you*.

It's an unwritten law. So many people I know found the real thing—not the flash-in-the-pan fling, but The One—only after they had reached the point where they could also be happy without ever finding him or her. For a lot of them, it took living alone and really coming to understand who they were and what they could offer someone else before they could be with that imaginary someone in a healthy and enduring way.

Maybe it will involve taking a course you always wanted to take. Or joining an athletic club. Or taking a trip.

Will that Japanese class help you find a partner? Will that skiing pass do it? Or driving cross-country with your best friend?

Maybe not, but you'll be out of the house and out of "waiting mode." You'll be getting on with your life and doing some of the things you've always wanted to do, rather than saving them for when you're "with someone."

In the process, you'll be discovering not just other people, but also the world and, most important, yourself.

Who you are.

What you like to do.

What you can offer.

You'll be learning to give, sometimes to friends and, by becoming the person you really want to be, to yourself.

That's the attractive force. It turns you into a magnet for others. It also makes you happier in the meantime.

And when a great one finally *does* cross your path and you're sitting across the table from each other, looking into each other's eyes, you'll feel ready, deserving, and up to the task, because you'll be an interesting person yourself: someone who makes things happen and has stories to tell.

CHAPTER 12

SETTING YOURSELF
UP TO SUCCEED

Expectations tend to be self-fulfilling.

—ANONYMOUS

*"Once I find her, I'll never be lonely again."*

*"She'll never look at another guy once she gets a load of me."*

*"He'll be rich and handsome."*

*"The sex will always be good."*

OKAY. NOW I'D LIKE TO come back down to planet Earth and discuss how to set yourself up to succeed, rather than fail, in relationships.

In Chapter 11, we touched on the idea that the quality of your life is up to you when you're single. But that's also true if you're with someone, so it's important to understand that a relationship won't solve your problems.

*"If it won't solve my problems, what's the point?"*

Just this: You'll get a lot farther if you keep in mind that, in or out of a relationship, your happiness and well-being are ultimately your own responsibility.

*"Whoa! Now you're saying a relationship won't make me happy, either?"*

It might. Special people tend to enhance our happiness. But there has to be a foundation for that happiness in the first place. In other words, if you don't have a capacity for making yourself happy, chances are someone else won't, either.

I'm not saying that you need to go into relationships problem free. No one's perfect. You're not; he or she isn't. But we need to be on guard against our natural tendency to think that our own problems are someone else's.

Let's take an imaginary guy, John, and use loneliness as an example. When John was single, he was always lonely.

He always assumed that when he found Ms. Right, he wouldn't ever feel lonely again. And that's a reasonable expectation, isn't it? He's thinking, *Whatever a relationship can or can't do, it should at least take care of loneliness, right?*

Well, not exactly. People in relationships are sometimes lonely, too.

The good news is that this sort of loneliness may be fixable. It might just be a question of John saying, "Katie, I think you're spending too much time with your friends," or his saying, "Katie, when we're having sex, new rule: *No texting.*"

And voilà. Problem solved.

But what if it goes deeper?

For example, what if John has a psychological leftover from when he was growing up? What if he's lonely because he's not able to fully give and receive love?

Whoa!

I know: big concept. But to say it another way, maybe he's shutting Katie out in some way, and that's why he feels lonely.

Is that her fault?

No.

Or what if John's in an ongoing struggle with his spiritual beliefs? He always wanted to believe in God but never quite could. Perhaps he stopped worrying about it when things started out hot and heavy with Katie, but now time has passed and that vague unfulfilled longing has crept back.

Her fault?

No.

Or what if—well, there are lots of ways people can feel lonely.

But whatever it is, it doesn't have to be a problem for the relationship. It doesn't need to separate them. John can figure out whatever it is and fix it.

Or, with her help, he can work it out.

No, it doesn't need to break them up *unless* John went into the relationship thinking, *She's supposed to cure my loneliness.*

So the key to his success is in whether he says, "I feel lonely again. I wonder where that's coming from?" or even "I wonder what I can do to change it?"

Rather than saying, "There's something wrong with Katie. She's not living up to her side of the bargain. She was supposed to keep me from ever feeling lonely again, and she isn't! I'd better get out of here."

We don't even say this kind of thing consciously. Sometimes we just *feel* it.

In this case, John's not even seeing that it was his problem to begin with.

So, the more self-aware he and she are, and the more realistic their expectations of each other are, the greater the chance it will work.

Or, to say it another way:

The less we expect our partners to fix our lives for us, the better our chances that our relationships will succeed.

❧

*"He spends too much time with his friends, but I'll change him."*

  *"She's too wild for me, but I'll change her."*

  *"He embarrasses me when we're out, but I'll change him."*

  *"She smokes, and I hate it, but I'll change her."*

A word of advice: You won't.

And you'll probably have a really frustrating time trying.

This is another area where you can set yourself up to fail . . . or succeed.

Think of it this way.

Imagine how a parent might want *you* to change.

*"You'd really be happier, Jen,"* your mom might say, *"if you cut your hair a different way."*

Or, *"You'd be happy if you dated Arnold Witherspoon."*

Or, *"If you pursued astrophysics."*

How does *that* feel?

Do you imagine yourself saying, *"Gee, Mom, you're right! I'll change my hair right away. What about the color? Should I change that, too?"*

Or would you more likely be thinking, *"@#$%!@#$!!"*?

Now, some people *do* listen to their parents' advice, and lots of parents are great about how they present that advice. But in general, when you try to tell someone else how to behave, it backfires.

Consider the fact that your "You need to change!" language may sound to your partner just like *a parent's voice.*

Scary, but true.

I know how it happens. One of the beautiful things about starting out in a new relationship is that you're open-minded. It's exciting, it feels good, you're on top of the world, and you think he or she would be *perfect* if only he or she changed one little thing.

Or three little things.

Or five.

And then it'll all be good.

Except perfection doesn't exist.

Not only that, but people are, to a large extent, how they're always going to be. This is one thing I've definitely learned over time. There are exceptions, of course—it may be that your girl-friend really will stop smoking someday. But a lot of us largely conduct our lives in the way we want to, and to hear from someone else that this isn't acceptable just creates bad feelings.

If *she* really wants to stop smoking, she'll try to quit, and she might succeed. But you can't make her, and if you're trying, and it's driving you crazy that she can't or won't, you need to take a big step back from the situation and ask yourself, "Why is this making me so unhappy?"

"What does it say about me?"

"Why do I need her to meet this expectation so badly?"

"If it bothers me so much, why did I choose someone who smokes?"

Have I, Ken, changed since getting married? Yes! But only in ways I was open to anyway. And there was really no way for my wife to know what those ways were beforehand. Essentially, she chose to marry someone whom she thought was more or less okay. And I did the same in choosing her.

I was quite different in my twenties, though. Back then, I
didn't worry about my long-term compatibility with the women
I chose to spend time with. And I thought change was easier, for
me and for anyone else, than I now understand it to be.

The moral of this story? Pick someone you don't feel the need
to change very much. You'll save yourself a lot of time and energy—
and both you and your partner will be happier in the long run.

☙

So how else can you set yourself up to succeed?

*Take people at their word.*

If early in a relationship someone says, even in a lighthearted
but potentially serious way, something like "I'm really selfish,"
you may:

A. Think to yourself, *She doesn't mean it. I bet she's
   not really selfish.*

B. Think, *It might be fun to stick around and find out if
   she's joking . . . or if I can change her!*

C. Turn to the waiter and say, "Check, please!"

Correct answer?

C.

Let's do another.

The guy you're having a drink with says, "I'm not up for a
relationship right now. I'm just having fun with lots of women
and don't really want to put all my eggs in one basket. But someday I'm sure it'll be different."

You can take this to mean:

A. He's on the verge of changing, and with gentle coaxing and patience, he might be convinced to change, and maybe even commit . . . *to you!*

B. He's not up for a relationship right now.

Correct answer?

**B.**

Next.

Someone says to you, "I always sabotage relationships" or "I'm trouble."

I think you can see where I'm going with this.

⊙♌

*"Once I find her, I'll never be sexually dissatisfied again."*

*"Sex will always be perfect and fulfilling with The One."*

Really? On what planet, again?

As relationships move from being new to being less new, sexual attraction changes.

Usually, it becomes less intense than it was in the beginning.

Does that mean you need to find someone else?

Well, if you were just in it for the sex, then yes.

But if you want to stay, you'll need to figure out how to keep the physical attraction exciting, as most long-term couples need to do.

Diminished attraction can also be a sign that the relationship needs work in *other* areas.

For example, let's say you're angry at your partner. Can that be resolved in bed?

Perhaps so, but I'd say that if you use sex to fix the problem, you'll change your general anger into:

1. A white-hot burning anger, or

2. A dull, permanent, subtly throbbing repulsion

It's nice to have choices, but, ummm, these are probably not the ones you were hoping for.

So the task would be to get rid of the anger first.

☙

*"When I'm with the right person, I'll never have to worry about money again."*

If you marry for money, you'll pay for it every day for the rest of your life.

I feel it's important to add, for good measure, that you can also marry someone with no money and be miserable. This is America, after all, and we're free to make our own choices.

But marrying for money doesn't usually work out the way one would anticipate.

☙

Okay. One last scenario.

*"When I'm in a relationship, I'll never feel the desire even to* look *at anyone else again, and neither will he (or she)!"*

Ahem.

Good one!

Moving on.

# CHAPTER 13

# FRIENDSHIP AS A MODEL

Your friend is the one who knows all
about you, and still likes you.

—ELBERT HUBBARD

I RECENTLY REESTABLISHED CONTACT WITH an old friend whom I hadn't seen for years. She was never a girlfriend, because each of us always seemed to be involved with someone else whenever the issue came up. So instead, we became the best of friends. We'd hang out, have lunch, sometimes go for drinks, and once we even went to Central Park and played catch with a baseball and gloves.

Years later, after we'd lived in different cities for a while, it was great to see her again, and it was easy to pick up where we'd left off.

At our reunion lunch, I asked her if she was still in touch with any of her ex-boyfriends or, for that matter, her ex-husband.

"Absolutely not," she said.

"Me neither," I said, even though I don't have an ex-husband.

We came to the conclusion that if *we* had been more than just friends back in our twenties, we'd be less likely to be in touch now.

Strange, yes?

I know. Some people *are* in touch with their exes. Which is great.

But a lot of people aren't.

Why?

Well, there are lots of reasons, many of them having to do with hurt feelings. But one possibility is that the two people involved never actually thought of each other as friends when they were together. So why would they try to be friends once it was over?

Here's the thing: A *really good* long-term relationship—one that might even last a lifetime—is more of a "best friendship" than anything else.

Why?

Well, to begin with, people can be very caught up in the heat of passion and very soon afterward be ready to get out. In other words, chemistry, no matter how powerful, isn't enough to sustain a long-term connection.

And it goes without saying that married people can grow to not like each other. You've heard what people say, usually when a family member is driving them crazy: "I love her, but I don't *like* her." Except in marriages, the "love" part can't be taken for granted. People feel more of an obligation to love their relatives. But this isn't so with a spouse. Familiarity can breed boredom and, well, annoyance. This is, in part, why the divorce rate is so high. Yet in an ideal world, you'd think that both "love" and "like" would be the very *least* we could expect a husband or wife to feel for his or her spouse.

So why do the best long-term relationships involve a kind of affection similar to the way we feel about best friends?

Or, to put it another way, what do we do with our friends that's different, and sometimes better, than what we do with our lovers?

For starters, how did you meet your best friend, or best friends? Did you go to a bar? I don't think so. You probably weren't even *trying* to meet anyone. You grew up together, or met at school or work, and then the connection grew naturally in the course of just living your life.

Some people conduct their friendships much more intensely than this—some people can be bossy and possessive even with their friends—but usually, in the very best and happiest friendships, there's a more organic, easygoing quality to how it begins and evolves.

The thing is, this is actually a good way to meet a partner. Not by "looking," but just by living your life. I call it "being in your power," by which I mean being focused primarily on trying to be the best person you can be, which often coincides with being at your happiest and most interesting. This will draw partners to you in much the same way that it draws friends.

Another difference between the way we approach friendship and the way we search for The One is this: Generally, we don't have to cover every base for our friends, nor do they need to do so for us.

We don't tend to think that any one friend has to satisfy all of our needs. With one of your friends, you might tend to be silly and laugh a lot; with another, you might share an interest in sports; with another, you might watch films and talk about "serious" stuff; and with another, you may do something else entirely.

Yet when we think of finding The One, the major boyfriend or girlfriend, husband or wife, we often think in terms of finding someone who'll cover all the bases.

While it's good to try to find someone who matches a lot of your needs and preferences, it's also helpful to realize that he's not going to cover every base. He won't always look right, won't always say the right thing, won't always do the right thing.

Basically, he won't be perfect. If you're expecting him to, he'll disappoint. And if he expects *you* to be perfect, *you'll* disappoint. And that disappointment eats away at love; eventually, it will even eat away at "like."

☙

Another difference between the way we treat our friends and the way we treat a significant other is that we don't usually try to change our friends. We've already talked about trying to change people (see Chapter 12), so I only have a little more to say here.

*"He's inconsiderate, but I'll change him."*

*"She's too wild for me, but I'll change her."*

Don't these two statements sound crazy in the context of friendship? Of course they do. Why? Because we know how to "live and let live" with friends. And frankly, we probably wouldn't initiate a friendship with someone we felt so strongly compelled to change.

Say your friend Alex tells dumb jokes. Or Josh eats food off your plate. You might get annoyed, but your attitude is probably not far from "Oh well, that's Alex" or "That's just Josh."

It's a little more complicated when you're married to Bill, and one day it occurs to you to say, "Excuse me, Bill, honey?"

"Yes?"

"I may have mentioned it before, but I thought you might want to know: Ummm . . . if you chew with your mouth open at dinner tonight, here's what I'm going to do. I'm going to wait until you fall asleep, drive to The Home Depot, buy an ice pick, come home, and thrust it through the soft part of your neck."

About that, I have three comments.

1. Welcome to life as a couple.

2. Find someone who chews the way you like before you marry him (or her).

3. Speaking for the male contingent: We're able to learn, say, not to leave the toilet seat up, but that's about it. Beyond that, try not to overload us.

And finally, I think I'd better add, for my own safety:

4. My wife, Bette, has perfect table manners, better than my own. It was a made-up example.

Okay, men do change a bit more than just by learning to keep the seat down. So do women. But people change slowly, and only if they intended to do so anyway, or in ways they choose for themselves. In friendship, for the most part, we appreciate that people only change in ways they wanted to anyway.

And yes, this is why quite often our friends continue liking us day after day, month after month, year after year, decade after decade. Because we like friends the way they are. We don't ask them to change, and they like us just fine as we are, too.

❧

So, back to where we began.

Some people need help in the friendship department as well, but for a lot of you, your friends are a very positive, low-maintenance, and relatively *easy* part of life.

Of course, when I say that you should model love relationships on friendships, I'm not advocating a "lesser" form of connection, like Relationship Lite. The truth is that serious relationships require a lot more work than friendships do. After all, you're with a partner more or less *all the time*. No person who's been married for years, even happily, is going to tell you it's a piece of cake.

But if you're trying to figure out how to have a successful long-term relationship and you already have some good long-time friends, then, probably much more than you realize, you already know how it works.

# CHAPTER 14

# BREAKUPS

If people don't want to come out to the
ballpark, nobody's going to stop them.

—YOGI BERRA

THERE'S AN OLD JOKE THAT Woody Allen tells in *Annie Hall*.

A guy goes to a psychiatrist and says,
"Doc, my brother's crazy. He thinks he's a chicken."

And the doctor says,
"Aren't you going to turn him in?"

And the guy says,
"No! I need the eggs."

Sometimes we get involved with the wrong person for the
wrong reasons, or even the right person for the right reasons.
Either way, there often comes a time when being with that
person is ultimately more painful than not being with him or
her. But we stay in the relationship anyway, because "we need
the eggs."

And eventually Life says, "It was just a joke. There are no
chickens or eggs here. Just people. People who are suffering
because they need to split up but they can't."

In friendships, we tend have a sense of boundaries, but in tighter connections like those we have with lovers, our boundaries often get trampled, and it hurts. Why? Because we hope so much that our "serious" relationships will work out. We've invested ourselves and our time in them, and we've come to *love* someone. But sometimes relationships just *can't* work out. Sometimes they *shouldn't* work out, even if we love someone. And this is the spirit in which we need to look at breakups.

∞

When I was in my twenties, I fell in love with a woman. To me, one of her most admirable qualities was her strength. Sometimes she could also be a very angry person, but this seemed related to her strength, so I accepted it. For my part, I *wasn't* a very strong person at the time, and this is probably why I admired her so much.

This woman liked me, too—a lot. But note the careful word selection: "liked," rather than "loved," the way people like yogurt, or Wednesdays. And we were together for a while, though it was long-distance for most of that time.

I couldn't imagine it lasting forever, to be truthful. I could see the writing on the wall.

And yet, I felt I was nothing without her.

Now, by staying in a relationship with her, I'd have remained what I was: the weaker half of a couple. But what I actually wanted was to be a stronger person.

So here's what happened: She dumped me. I was devastated—I felt like I'd been punched in the stomach, and it took me a long time to get over it. But in the agony of the breakup, I got stronger.

So actually, the biggest tragedy of my life at the time was ultimately . . . a success.

But if someone had said to me at the time, "Okay, Ken, here's the deal. You can (A) go through this breakup now and it will really hurt, and she'll be out of your life forever—but it will probably make you stronger, or (B) stay with her for a few more weeks, maybe even months. You won't change very much in the meantime—but you'll still be with the woman you love, for a while."

I'd have chosen B.

I would have had a flag printed up with the words "I'LL STILL BE WITH HER FOR A WHILE, ALL RIGHT?" and carried it around.

Well, maybe not.

But I'd have wanted to stay. *I'd have stayed.*

Fortunately, or unfortunately, life has a way of making these choices for us.

And years later, when my wife-to-be arrived on the scene, and I needed to be stronger for this new relationship than I was at 25, I *was* stronger.

The earlier relationship prepared me. Actually, it was the *breakup* that prepared me. The breakup, though not as pleasant as the memories of the hot, fun, dramatic moments of the relationship we shared, was what gave me the biggest long-term benefit.

This is another good way to understand a breakup: as part of the relationship. It's nice when it happens gracefully—however rarely that occurs—but either way, the breakup teaches us lessons. Sometimes they're the most valuable ones.

⌒⌒

A friend recently told me that he and a woman he'd been with for years had ended it, and he was heartbroken. *She'd* betrayed *him* with another guy and given him a reason to go! Now, months later, she wanted him back and said she couldn't live without him. She was so down that he'd been phoning her mother because he still worried about her.

But he didn't want to go back.

He felt that the relationship had grown stale before all the drama, anyway. Now they'd practically destroyed each other, and he felt that the path forward, for each of them, was separate.

It seems to me that relationships give us certain hoops to jump through, like the hoops lions have in the circus. Those hoops are designed specifically for us and are as unique as our fingerprints. We don't choose them, they choose us.

Once we see what the hoop is, our best choice is to say, "Yes. I'll jump." If we refuse, we'll probably just have to deal with the same hoop in another time and place, anyway.

Same hoop, different person. People often marry a new version of a previous companion. Why? Because we each have issues to resolve, and leaving the first person doesn't always mean we've resolved them. So life sets it up for us again. "Learn the lesson—this is your second chance."

We love the people we love, yes. And my friend loved this woman. But sometimes it's better for both people if they continue to love each other from a distance—in their prayers, maybe, or even just occasionally in their thoughts.

What were the hoops? Maybe *letting go of a stale relationship,* jumping through the hoop of independence—which is a statement to yourself and the world: I'll find a *new* dynamic with someone else.

Or perhaps you could call it the hoop of *not staying together out of guilt;* of bravely trusting that life will bring each of you whatever new experiences—and people—you're meant to encounter.

❧

I tend to look at these situations creatively.

For example, my friend and the woman who betrayed him were together off and on, over and over, which is like a relationship with its own traffic light. That was their pattern.

But what my friend really desired—or at least what he told me he really wanted—was a connection that could grow and last. An open road, with no obligation to keep stopping all the time.

So, to accept that his life was supposed to go on without this woman, he might think of it this way.

> *She was good for me for a while, but now life wants me to understand who I am without her.*

> *My self-esteem is so low I can walk on it, but when I find it again, it will be more substantial than it was before. And I need to earn it alone.*

> *She says she can't live without me, so she probably needs to, well, live without me. No one can be a crutch for anyone else. Her lost self-esteem is hers to earn back, too.*

*She gets to be alone now, and she'll learn what she needs to—in her time, in her way.*

*If I can accept that I'm supposed to go on without her, mourning the pain, sending her my good thoughts but believing in my better future, I'll be happier. And I'll start attracting better people, people I can't even imagine yet.*

Now that I think of it, my friend's hoop looks a lot like the one I had to jump through after my strong-angry woman dumped me.

And?

My wife is worth everything I went through—and 10 times more.

⌇

I was once in the Florida Everglades with my then-girlfriend, and we decided to paddle a canoe into alligator-infested waters. I guess this was "interesting" and "fun."

Now I think of it somewhat differently—kind of like this: *What the @#$%! were we thinking?* But actually, I remember that it was really beautiful, being one with nature. (In this case, "being one with nature" sounded like "Is the alligator here yet?" I'll tell you, it really clears your mind, focuses your concentration, and chills you out on the smaller stuff when alligators are actually swimming under your canoe.)

Anyway, before we shoved off, the guy at the dock said, "Don't let your hands drift in the water, but besides that, don't worry too much—because to the alligators, you two and the boat are one huge creature. They'll avoid you."

I got it. I wasn't just me. I was *me, my girlfriend, and the boat.*

But here's the thing: Just like alligators confuse the boat and the two people in it for one entity, in waning relationships, we often lose track of what's ours and what belongs to the person we won't be with anymore.

When you go through a breakup, you'll tend to fear that love itself, for you, is over. And that can be terrifying. But if you love someone, you'll probably continue loving that person in a way, at least for a while, and maybe even forever. That doesn't mean that you and your partner need to still be together for you to express it. You don't need to make him or her *feel* that love, and, by the obvious terms of the breakup, you'll need to learn to understand this on your own.

If she loved you before, beneath any possible anger she may feel now, she still probably feels something—if that's any consolation. But in a sense, what she does or does not still feel for you won't change the fact that she may want to love someone else.

Ouch.

I know.

But you will, eventually, want to love someone else, too.

As for your ability to love, you need to remember that it isn't cut off by your not being with her (or him). Your ability to love is real and powerful. It's a force like the sun—which, by the way, was made to light more than one planet. The next step is to realize that this ability to love is a gift. It can take you far. Eventually, it will take you to someone else, someone better for you.

So if the agony you feel is "She was the only one for me; she's so special," which is usually a version of "No one else will love me," wait a minute.

Stop right there.

And remember: *That's* you . . . and *that's* the boat. Separate.

She isn't the goddess of love, and love doesn't work that way.

He isn't the god of love. *It doesn't work that way!*

Let's take it one step further.

Think of it like this: That relationship probably allowed you to keep certain inner belief systems hidden, or stalled.

So what is the hoop for you to jump through?

Maybe it's "If I let him go, I'd have to grow up."

Or "If I let her go, I'd have to stop depending on someone else to make me happy. I'd have to find my own happiness."

Or "If let him go, I'll have to deal with my responsibility for all of this. Why did I choose someone like that?"

Or "If I let her go, I'll have to deal with why I'm not a happy person."

We drag our feet because we don't want to confront these big issues. So try to think of the breakup as the universe talking to you. What's it saying?

"Hey, you. It's time to figure out a few things and *grow*."

That's part of the relationship's gift: Its end.

I know.

It's hard to become someone new. It's hard to grow.

Why?

Because life is a series of patterns, and, like our green, scaly friends who swim under canoes, we tend not even to see what they are, never mind think about breaking them.

We don't say, "This is me" and "This is my pattern." We just say, "This is how life is."

Here are a couple of examples of how "life is."

For Person A: Women can't be trusted.

For Person B: Men always leave.

For Person B, it's not about how her father was, or a boyfriend, or even two boyfriends. To her, it's how *all* men are.

So what happens next?

Well, she might attract a man who leaves.

Why would she do that? There's a good quote about that one:

> How many pessimists end up by desiring
> the things they fear, in order to prove that
> they are right?
> —*Robert Mallet*

Or, to take Person A, he might attract a woman who's untrustworthy.

Sound crazy?

In psychology, it's a whole field: object relations. It's why people who were physically abused by their parents often find themselves in physically abusive relationships with their partners. It's all they know. We don't try to do it. We just tend to seek out and attract people who conform to our understanding of how the world is.

It might look bad from the outside. For example, abuse is bad; we all know that. But if you grow up with it, you think, *This is just how relationships are.* And you go out and find similar situations. Or they find you.

Gulp.

Is there any good news here?

Yes.

You know how much pressure it takes to convert a piece of coal into a diamond? Lots.

And when we're in a bad breakup, we feel agony, frustration, despair—and these are forms of pressure. In other words, even though it's hard to see our patterns, and it's really hard to move past them, breakups are an opening; they're an opportunity to change the coal of our ruts into the diamonds of who we want to be.

Let's say that before his breakup, a guy, Sean, thought *Women are untrustworthy.*

Why did he believe it in the first place? Maybe his father always said it. Or his mother lied to him a lot. Or, poor guy, it could have been something as small as the kindergarten teacher he loved so much moving to another school system halfway through the year without saying good-bye to her class.

And then, in college, Sean gets together with a woman who ultimately cheats on him. They break up.

Now he's in agony.

But while he mourns the loss of that relationship, he may wonder, *Is it true that all women are untrustworthy?*

And suddenly, because of the sheer force of his despair he may think, *I don't have time for clichés anymore. I don't care about how "all women" are.*

Instead, even in his pain, he'll ask himself, for the first time, "What do I need to learn here?"

"Did I attract this situation?"

"How can I do this differently next time?"

"How can I choose differently next time?"

"How can I change my life?"

Then he can go out, see his friends, and try to feel better.

And then, when he's alone again, he can ask himself these questions again and again.

And yes, he may find that he can actually grow out of the old belief.

And this would be a gift from the breakup.

❦

Breakups happen, and sometimes they really hurt.

But, understood correctly, they can be a time of shedding old beliefs.

If you let them, breakups will lead you to something better: to becoming the person you really want to be.

# PART 3

# PARENTS

CHAPTER 15

GETTING IT RIGHT

*Man's main task in life is to give birth to himself.*

—ERICH FROMM

THIS SECTION IS ABOUT YOU and your parents.

*"Oh God. Do I really have to deal with that?"*

Yes, you do.

In a big way.

We all do.

Why?

Because failing to deal with your parents can sabotage other important aspects of your life. I've seen it so many times. Trust me on this one. It can stand in the way of your happiness, success, and yes, even true love.

Your relationship with your parents probably falls into one of the following categories.

## CATEGORY 1

You're really close to your parents; best friends, even. You and your parents actually enjoy one another and almost always see eye to eye.

Lucky you.

Run with it.

## CATEGORY 2

There's loads of love between you, but sometimes your parents drive you crazy. (I see that most people have raised their hands. You can put them down now.)

Still, lucky you. Walk with it—because this is a pretty good place to be. You aren't best friends with your parents—maybe not even by a long shot—but you're trying to get things right.

## CATEGORY 3

You and your parents aren't close at all. You may not even be in touch with them, nor do you want to be. Or perhaps one of your parents isn't in touch with *you*. Maybe one of them mistreated you. Maybe your parents went through an acrimonious divorce and forced you to choose a side.

It's still important to get things right, though—if not with them, at least in your own mind.

I'm going to start with you.

☙

I once attended a weekend seminar on a lake in the mountains. We took frequent breaks, and I'd usually head outside to sit by the water. I met a young woman who was there with her mother. She sat in on a few lectures, but mostly she just swam in the lake or sat on the shore.

She told me that her parents were divorced. She said that she didn't see or speak to her father. She didn't "deal with him" anymore.

Over the course of the weekend, we spoke a handful of times, and each time she managed to bring up her father and say the same thing, and always with conviction in her voice. The words changed a little each time, but not their message: "I don't deal with him anymore."

Finally, at our last meeting, I said, "You know, you *do* deal with him."

"What do you mean?" she asked.

"You've made him a part of all our conversations."

That's the thing. Remember how I said that if you don't deal with your parents, that failure to deal can easily get in the way of everything else?

This is important.

All of us struggle with someone close to us at some point in our lives. It's part of being human. (That means you, too, Category 1!) Humans, when they interact with one another, experience friction, plain and simple. If we didn't, we would be machines: thoughtless, emotionless robots. (And not much fun on a date, besides.)

So if this girl didn't want to see her father, maybe she was right. Frankly, I never asked her what happened, so I can't judge. But she *still* needs to come to a peaceful understanding *in her own head* to be truly free.

How will she know she has succeeded? Well, if she finds that when she thinks about her father she feels, for the most part, calm and free to pursue her own goals—mission accomplished. But if the thought of her father provokes anger or anxiety, or if she finds herself frequently distracted by negative thoughts of him, then she still has work to do. That work might involve actual communication with her father, but then again, it might not. It might be more private: a change in her own habits and a kind of mental "letting go."

For most people, it's not this extreme. But the same principles apply. Even if your parents drive you crazy for no particular reason, it's still in your best interests to try to get the situation "right."

I know, "letting go" and getting something "right" sound mysterious and maybe even impossible. There's no Get It Right with My Parents button you can simply push and be done with it. But there are specific actions you can take—and in the next few chapters, we'll discuss a lot of them.

For now, the thing to remember is that you really do have a lot of power to change your relationship with your parents for the better, and the sooner you take steps in this direction, the sooner you'll feel more peaceful and confident in other areas, too.

It often begins when you're living at home.

CHAPTER 16

# HOME AGAIN

The art of being wise is the art of knowing what to overlook.

—WILLIAM JAMES

YOU'VE BEEN ON YOUR OWN for years, coming and going as you like, and not having to answer to anyone.

Then school ends, and—like a lot of new grads, especially these days—you move back home until you can find a job and save enough money to get a place of your own.

Suddenly, your parents—who now seem to be in bed by 9 o'clock each night—want to know what time you'll be coming home, where you're going, and whom you're with. Suddenly, you're a kid all over again—and you might even have the twin bed to prove it. It's as if a time machine whisked you back to the past but forgot to come back to pick you up.

Are there any easy solutions?

You could write a letter.

Dear Time Machine,

I get it. You've put me back in my old life. Good one! Well played! Now could you please work your magic again in the opposite direction and find me a cool

living space and a great job—ideally one that pays for
my cool living space?

Yours Truly,

You

But where would you send it?

☙

There has to be another way to approach this.

Let's start here: Moving back in with one or both of your
parents can make you feel like a failure, even if your friends are
in the same boat. Like a boomerang, your sailing back to where
you started can seem to bode badly for your ability to make it
in the world. *If only I'd gotten a job,* you may be thinking, *making a good salary.* Or *If I only knew what I wanted to do and
could figure out how to do it, I wouldn't have to live with my
parents!*

Let's nip this one in the bud.

As I've mentioned before, the biggest misconception after
graduating from college is that you'll get a job right away. When
you don't, despair often sets in.

*But this could be true whether you're living at home again
or not.*

It's easy to shift the blame for that despair: "I'm upset
*because I'm at home.*"

But this probably isn't really the case. Living at home again
can be challenging, yes, but if you can work it to your advantage, it will go down in your history as A Smart Move.

*"Fine,"* you say. *"But what about my parents treating me like I'm still in high school?"*

Okay. Imagine throwing an apple as high as you can into the air. What happens next?

Gravity pulls it down again, of course.

When you move back home, you feel vulnerable to a similar kind of gravity. You're the apple, and college launched you really high into your own freedom. Now, sitting on your old bed again, waiting for dinner—if you're lucky enough to have someone making it for you—you feel a tremendous weight pulling you back into all the old patterns. You feel like a loser? Well, who *didn't* feel like a loser sometimes growing up? And now you're back at the scene of the crime!

As far as landing your first job is concerned, we've already talked about lots of ways to get some momentum going. Now we need to do something similar with your parents. How can you manage the situation so it doesn't become its own quicksand of frustration and despair?

Let's break it down.

A friend once told me that when she moved back home after college, she found herself constantly closing the door to her bedroom and spending as much time as possible hiding out there—just like when she was a teenager. Her parents always wanted to know what she was doing. When she'd go out, she found herself

inventing excuses to stay out longer. She felt like a failure, child-
ish and miserable.

Maybe your situation isn't as bad as hers. Maybe in your
case, you feel old frictions and pressures, but you're able to deal
with these and not let them drag you down. Good!

For those who feel like this woman did, however, I'll say a
bit more.

The ideal would be to establish boundaries that you can all
live with. An "I'll do this, and we'll agree on that" type of thing.
Parents may not always be receptive or reasonable, but this is
the ideal, so let's talk about pursuing it.

Where do you begin?

You want to be treated like an adult.

But being treated like an adult requires exhibiting adultlike
behavior. And one of the hallmarks of maturity is understanding and participating in "two-way streets."

So your mother worries about what time you'll be home.
This can be annoying, yes. It might even be completely unreasonable of her. But consider that if she's taking it way too far, it
may be partly because being aware of what time you get in at
night is as much a burden to her as it is to you. Maybe she slept
more soundly when you were away. Maybe she didn't panic
every time a police siren went off in the neighborhood, thinking
you had just been mowed down by a truck—but now she does.
Or maybe she was *just* as nervous about you when you were
away, and seeing you every day makes it hard for her to resist
expressing it now, no matter how hard she tries. A two-way
negotiation involves considering not only your frustrations and
how easy it is to fall back into old patterns, but also her predica-
ment, as well. Is this hard to do? Yes, it is. I know.

The truth is, you're probably not the only "apple." The gravity that comes with reverting to an old situation might be pulling your parents back into *their* old patterns, too. And you were probably not the only one who felt freer when you were away—and this may be so even if your siblings are still at home. Not that your parents don't love you and want to be with you (don't go feeling guilty on me now—that's not where I'm going with this); it's just important to bear in mind that they, too, are being forced into a slightly odd position. The time machine has taken them back to the past, too. Starting from *that* mentality may make it easier to meet them somewhere in the middle.

If this were a perfect world, you'd just say, "Mom, Dad, get over worrying about what time I'll be home. I'm an adult. Treat me like one"—and they'd do it. But if they've been dragged back into their own old patterns, it may be hard for them to make the jump. After all, they weren't at college to see how well you handled yourself.

And they might also be thinking, not unfairly, *Adults don't get free (or reduced) rent.* Which is a point. When you're depending on someone, you have to accept that it may come at a price. And if you're not yet in a position to pay for a place of your own, then for maturity's sake, not to mention your own peace of mind, you need to put yourself in the shoes of your landlords. Try to be more understanding of the compromises they're making, as well—even if it doesn't seem they're doing the same for you.

It's hard, I know. Sometimes it even spirals out of control, and everyone starts shouting. One of you is thinking, *I'm definitely right,* and the other one is thinking, *I'm definitely right,* so you're deadlocked, and there's lots of huffing and puffing.

Don't worry. I'm going to discuss how to deal with this in the coming chapters.

For now, keep in mind that there's an obvious upside to living at home, or you wouldn't have even considered it: Living at home gives you the chance to explore career possibilities with less financial pressure.

So it's important to make the most of that chance.

Remember the woman who found herself staying in her room and always shutting the door? She managed to live with her parents for a year, and only after moving out was she able to acknowledge that there was something *smart* and *responsible* about her decision to live at home.

She wanted to work at an art gallery, but she was finding it difficult to get her foot in the door. Living rent free enabled her to take a modest-paying job as a waitress in a café *connected* to the art gallery where she wanted to work. After a few months, she was hired to be communications coordinator of the gallery itself. It turned out to be a dream job for her at the time—and once she got it, she was also able to get a place of her own.

This woman insists today that she never would have been hired for the art gallery job based on her major and résumé alone. But once she was in the café, the owners came to like and appreciate her intelligence, good character, and strong people skills. And that was how they came to realize that she was the person they needed.

I know it sounds like a hard way to get there. After all, who but aspiring actors, artists, and maybe restaurant owners plans to wait tables after graduation? And will just *any* job lead to such a prize opening? Not necessarily, no. It doesn't always begin all that easily in the working world. (If you live at home, it may seem that it doesn't begin all that easily at all!) But with the little bit of financial flexibility living at home affords you, you might stand a better chance of finding or creating just the right opportunity for yourself.

⌘

So remember: You are *not* a failure for living at home.

If possible, come to an understanding with your parents. Try to think of them not just as your parents, but also as adults, with frustrations and desires, just like you. Growing up also means growing *out*—for your parents, as well. Everyone will probably be more at ease when you're on your own.

But you still need to try to think of living at home as part of the solution. It's a contributor to, rather than a drag on, your forward momentum.

Don't lose sight of your goal: working for the life you really want.

# CHAPTER 17

# CAREER CHOICES, FAMILY STYLE

Do not do unto others as you would that they should do unto
you. Their tastes may not be the same.

—GEORGE BERNARD SHAW

AND WHAT HAPPENS WHEN YOUR parents have one idea for
your career and you have another?

Are they right?

Are you?

A reporter for the *Wall Street Journal* once wrote about how
parents tend to give their children career advice based on how
things were for *them,* back when *they* were first entering the
workforce. [1]

In other words, it's probably quite a bit like the advice they
wish someone had given them.

If you're in your early twenties and have no idea of what to
do, or if you do have an idea, but you're not sure (join the club—
it's a big one), you'll probably need to figure it out through trial
and error. So it's hard to expect anyone else, even a parent, to
know the answer in advance.

The thing to remember is that a parent wants you to be
happy and successful. Your parents' intentions in giving advice

are usually the best. They mean well. It may *feel* like their only objective in life is to control you, but it usually isn't. Trust me on that one.

At the same time, a parent will be advising you based on two factors, both of which are, by their very nature, subjective.

1. Who your parent is. Her *own* history and aspirations.

2. Your parent's understanding of you.

So how does this play out in reality?

Well, it's easiest for everyone when #1 and #2 are in perfect sync.

For example, your mother—who may have always wanted to be a doctor herself but instead stayed home to raise her children—may say, "*I* think medicine's a great field. All my doctor friends are happy and respected and successful. And it would make me proud to tell people you're a doctor. More important, it seems to me that *you* would be a happy and successful doctor, because you like biology, you like chemistry, you like helping people, and you were really good with Grandpa when he was in the hospital last spring. So my advice would be that medicine might be a good area for you to pursue."

Assuming you hadn't already told your mother umpteen times that you absolutely, under any circumstances, categorically DO NOT WANT TO BE A DOCTOR, I would say she handled this little moment pretty well, even though a bit of self-interest crept in. That's natural. Grade: √+

When #1 and #2 are *not* in sync, however, things can get a bit tricky.

Let's pretend you're my child.

"Dad," you wander in and say. "I really love cooking. I think maybe I should go to culinary school and become a chef. Whadda ya think?"

So I reflect on that, inevitably bringing my own experiences into the equation. I'm thinking:

I *always wanted to be a* doctor, *but I never had the guts to do it. And having my child be a doctor would probably make me feel proud. Not only that, but doctors make pretty good money, and money is something I don't ever want my son to worry about—I want him to be really happy and secure—so there's another plus for doctors. . . .*

"Dad?" you say.

"One minute. I'm thinking. Can you give me a minute?"

"Sure."

And then I think, *This guy I knew in high school, Jarrett Martin, became a successful doctor, and guess what? He ended up marrying Lori, this beautiful girl who dumped me in 10th grade.*

"Uh, Dad? Hey! You there?"

"Sorry!" I finally say. "Here's the thing. What about medicine? Do you have any interest in medicine? Any at all?"

"It's okay, I guess."

"Well, I think it would be a good field for you."

My grade as a parent: √-.

I was considering the question from my perspective, but then my perspective is limited. As is everyone's.

But what was my intent? A kind and loving one. I wanted you to be happy and successful. And again, for the vast majority of you, this is what your real parents want for you, as well.

The point here is that parents give the best advice they can, but they don't always realize that it may not be the best advice for that particular case.

Remembering this will make a big difference in conversations you have with your parents about your prospective career. If anyone's speaking from a defensive, suspicious, or angry place, the only thing guaranteed to come out of that conversation is more frustration, resentment, and anger.

All of which are a waste of time. After all, you need a job!

Let's pick up where we left off, with me standing in for your dad again.

"Why do you want me to be a doctor?" you ask.

"Because doctors make a good living, and it's a noble profession."

The thing is, this isn't what Ken/Dad is *really* saying. What he's *really* saying isn't "Be a doctor—or else!" It's this:

"Live comfortably, do good, and be happy."

Which is pretty much what everyone wants, isn't it? Doesn't that sum up what you want for yourself?

When you look at it this way, maybe you can see the spirit behind "my" motivations a little bit more evenly, and maybe "I" will seem less like a doctor-wannabe whose sole interest lies in controlling you. I assure you this is not where "I'm" coming from.

It's probably not where your real father and mother are coming from, either.

Now let's focus on what I'm really saying—not "I want you to be a doctor" but, on a deeper level, "I want you to be successful and happy." Here are some possible replies from you.

"Dad, listen. To be successful and happy at it, I'd need to really want to be a doctor, and the truth is, I don't."

"Not all doctors make buckets of money—and in any case, I'm less concerned with making money than with spending my time in a gratifying way."

"If I don't at least check out what it's like to be a chef, I'm afraid I'll always regret not trying something that I think could *really* make me happy."

Now, if I heard you say any one of these things in a thoughtful, respectful manner to *me,* I'd be pretty hard-pressed to object.

I'd remember the article I once read about the actress Diane Lane. Her father was an acting coach who put her on the stage at age 7. By the time she was a teenager, she was performing alongside Meryl Streep. She said her father dared her to "make it," which she did. But years later, having become a successful actress, she said she still wondered occasionally about what she might have done instead, and whether doing something other than what her father chose for her would have made her happier.

I'd also remember the time a friend who was a lawyer told me that his son didn't want to follow him into law, and that they'd fought about it.

Mostly, though, I'd remember my own story. *My* father had wanted me to be a commercial banker. At the time, I hadn't been able to think of a better plan, and, as a result, I spent years in the profession. It served an important function for me, yet the fact remains: I don't believe I ever could have risen to the top of the banking industry. Why? Because I wasn't sufficiently interested in commercial banking to apply myself the way people who make it to the top do.

So in this sense, my father didn't understand that his advice to be a commercial banker was at cross-purposes with what he really wanted for me: success. And with this in mind, I told my lawyer friend, "You don't have the power to lead your son to success as a lawyer, because *he's* the one who'll have to get out of bed every day and make it happen."

My friend's son ended up choosing his own direction, and now he and his father have worked it all out, and much more.

Now, as we know, I'm not your parent. And maybe one or both of your parents just aren't ready—and may never be ready—to accept your career decision. They might object, and maybe even in a manner that's far from calm or respectful. In that case, I would urge you to try to keep your cool and excuse yourself from the discussion, at least for the moment.

Maybe they'll come to their senses. Maybe they won't. But if you've heard them out and civilly stated your own case based on the best judgment you can muster at the time, you can feel some peace in knowing that you've done your best. You've made your case respectfully, which is a good thing to do for you, and a great courtesy to them.

And now you can . . . apply to culinary school.

⊙೫

I have one more scenario to discuss.

Someone else I know grew up with parents whose career advice boiled down to this: "Whatever you want to do is fine with us. We love you and will support whatever decision you make."

Hmm.

Some of you are probably thinking, *Wow. That's great. If only* my *parents were like that, I could get on with trying to be a writer/dancer/painter/philosopher/circus clown in peace.*

But think about it. Sometimes exactly what we need in order to figure out what we *really* want to do (or, for that matter, what we really *don't* want to do) is a little resistance.

My friend eventually did become a writer, and a successful one at that, but for a long time the utter freedom and encouragement to decide what she "truly wanted to be" had her flailing. Total freedom made her feel paralyzed with indecision.

This is not to say that her parents were to blame. On the contrary, their unconditional support is in no small part why she's able to do what she does now. The point is that without your realizing it, your parents may actually be saving you time by helping you rule out (or in) certain vocations.

The reality is that you're going to encounter a lot of people who will try to advise you on how to live your life, and these dealings won't always be harmonious. Dealing with your parents is kind of like a rehearsal; it's an opportunity for you to master similar situations with others.

How?

By holding on to what's good, keeping things calm and respectful as best you can, and staying true to your beliefs.

---

[1] Erin White, "Parents Don't Always Know Best about Jobs," *Wall Street Journal,* April 5, 2005, http://online.wsj.com/article/SB111265381581497689-search.html?collection=wsjie%252F30day&vql_string=erin+white%253Cin%253E(article-body)

# CHAPTER 18

# APPROVAL

The thing you have to be prepared for is that other people
don't always dream your dream.

—LINDA RONSTADT

IT'S NATURAL TO WANT A parent's approval. We all need it on
some level. And, over the years, I've noticed that those who have
it tend to feel better about themselves than those who don't.

Or, to say it another way, those who don't have it have to
work harder to achieve the same level of self-esteem.

Yet here's the simple truth about approval.

1. Parents aren't always able to give it to us in every
   area.

2. If they aren't, we have to seek it elsewhere, starting,
   of course, with ourselves.

3. The art of self-approval involves not just saying it,
   but also finding a way to feel it.

4. Not doing this is a way of shooting yourself in the
   foot.

Let's start with the idea that parents aren't always able to offer their approval in the areas we most want them to endorse.

Say you are a parent, and your neighbor, a former star athlete, is now a gung ho high school coach. He's pushing his son to excel in sports, but his child has a physical disability and an artistic bent. He hates watching sports on TV; he enjoys playing the guitar. Period.

You know from another neighbor that Jack, the father, almost made it to the Olympics, and now he's living through his kid. You hear them fighting from time to time, Jack saying, "This disability doesn't need to hold you back!" and the kid replying, "But I have no interest."

What would you do?

Hard to say.

You might try to talk to Jack, but what if he tells you it's best not to treat little Sam like a victim. "Remember Ray Charles?" he asks you. "He was blind, but his mother made him do everything for himself. Look how far he got!"

You're thinking, *Right. Ray Charles. He was blind, independent, and* wanted to be a musician.

"Anyway," Jack says, his face closer to yours, "you got a problem with how I'm raising my kid?"

Yikes.

But here's the point: If the "kid" in question is someone else's, you can see pretty clearly that being pushed in the wrong direction by his father isn't helping any.

But now what if it's your parent, doing it to you?

Trying to make you play ball, but you don't want to.

Wanting you to date one of your obnoxious cousin's friends, but you don't want to.

Or wanting you to be an engineer, but you're not interested.

Even if you say, "No, thank you," your instinctual need for your parent's approval might mean that in some way, shape, or form, you're considering options that you don't want.

But at some point you have to just tell yourself, *That's my mom's thing [or my dad's thing], not mine.*

And feel your creative energy return.

꩜

The need for approval is natural, but not always easy.

I know a woman who told me that after her parents' divorce, her father was always rude to her. She says she tried really hard, well into her twenties, to please her dad—but that he simply wouldn't connect. Finally, she gave up.

What she said to me was, "I realized the only person I needed to please was myself. If you need to seek approval, ask yourself if you're happy. If yes, then you already have approval from yourself; you just don't know it. It's much easier to suck it up and be an adult, to understand that things are not always fair, and people are not always going to pay attention to the good things you do in life because they're wrapped up in themselves."

She has a good point. Her life and her prospects for happiness would have been stalled if she'd just waited around for her father's approval instead of patting herself on the back and moving on.

In other words, she parented herself. That's very different from pretending that we don't need approval at all. The need for approval is real. The good news is, if you're not getting it, you can find it elsewhere: from friends, mentors, teachers,

other relatives—in short, from the whole gamut of feedback
you get as a result of your actions in the world. But the approval
of others is a subjective and unreliable game, so it remains useful to be able to supply it to yourself.

❦

Giving yourself the approval you need isn't easy. Why? Because
we often internalize and hold on to our parents' comments and
attitudes. If your mother repeatedly tells you that you're over-
weight, it can be hard not to believe her. If your father repeatedly says you're lazy, you probably think, *He's right. I probably
won't amount to much.*

Let's say my father has just called me lazy. I can tell myself,
"Ken! You're not lazy, you're great!" Saying it is one thing, but
in order to really feel better, I need to find a way to *convince*
myself that I'm not lazy.

And how do I do that?

By taking action.

So let's say you've been unemployed for months and then
you finally score an interview, but it's "just" an informational
one. Congratulations! Seriously. The task is to allow yourself to
actually feel good about this accomplishment, even if it doesn't
turn into your dream job. That positive reinforcement will help
you change the way you feel about yourself.

So how do you feel good about it?

Maybe you'll arrange a drink with a friend and a toast to
the achievement. Or go shopping for something new—even a
small thing. It's up to you to decide exactly how to celebrate—
just make sure that you do! Why? Because an informational

interview is a good thing. An informational interview means that something is happening in your life. But to have it make a dent in your beliefs about yourself, you have to take it in emotionally, rather than just as a piece of information.

The bottom line: Changing your beliefs about yourself involves manufacturing your own inspiration, a talent well worth cultivating.

❦

A final word about approval: Most parents sacrifice a lot for their children—time, energy, freedom, and money. That's a big part of what it means to be a parent—making sacrifices.

Now that you're an adult, if you continue to need approval in an area that your parents find difficult to understand, it's a bit like asking them to continue to parent you. If you can liberate your parents from this "obligation" to approve of your decisions—to see things exactly as you see them, or to be an expert on something they don't know enough about—you will liberate yourself, as well.

It's a generous act toward them, and even more so toward yourself.

CHAPTER 19

———— ✆ ————

# BLAME

When you blame others, you give up your power to change.

—DOUGLAS ADAMS

ONE OF YOUR GOALS IN life is to become the person you want to be. To approve of *yourself.*

And the secret about blame is this: It will slow you down.

Of course, blame is not just about parents; it can be about anyone. But it usually begins with parents, because it's with our parents that we form our earliest, closest relationships. If blaming is a part of the human condition, blaming our parents for our obstacles is a good place to start this discussion.

⊙ఠ

It's easy to think that blame is justified. Maybe a parent (or a friend) doesn't understand you, or doesn't stand behind you, or abuses you, or pressures you to do something you don't want to do.

*"And if someone shoves me, it's natural to get angry, isn't it?"*

Yes, it is. And being treated badly, even in a nonphysical

way, can often feel like being shoved. Blame is a natural and sometimes even protective response.

But only to an extent.

The question is, what do you do with blame?

How long do you hold on to it?

Here's the thing: Your life is your responsibility, not anyone else's. Blaming is the act of holding someone else responsible for whatever's wrong. And the crazy thing, the key, is that a big part of that last statement is "holding someone." Don't do it! If someone isn't treating you right, the last thing you want to do is hold on to that person or situation.

Of course, we like to think we can have our cake and eat it, too: that we can blame *and* get free of whatever it is we're angry about. We can blame them *and* not "hold" them. But what if it doesn't work that way? What if we're dealing with an either/or situation, and to be truly free, we have to let it go, meaning, let the other person off the hook?

Consider this: If someone said to you, "I think you're an idiot," would you reply: "Do you really? Cool. How about this: Every day for a week, let's meet, and each time I want you to say it again, that you think I'm an idiot."

I don't think so.

Yet when we blame, this is basically what we're doing: allowing ourselves to relive the insult again and again.

*Why would we?*

For one thing, blaming someone can feel active and productive, like moving along a path toward justice or revenge.

It makes you feel like you're moving toward making things right.

Believe me, I get it. I've done it.

But the bigger picture is this: We're each in a race to become the person we want to be: free, capable, effective, happy. Blame is like slowing down to trip up someone else—and tripping yourself in the process.

As William H. Walton once said, "To carry a grudge is like being stung to death by one bee."

There's another way to look at the same thing. Have you ever heard the expression "We're either part of the problem or part of the solution?" I like that one, because it implies that there's no middle ground. We have to come down on one side or the other.

Blame is the same way. To have the life you want, you need to leave your baggage behind and focus 100 percent of your energy on the future. The past is over, which means it's out of your control. The future is where solutions lie—and to an extent, you *can* control the future. So the ideal is to put the world of what went wrong behind you and move on to the world of the right.

⌘

*"Exactly how do I do this?"* you ask.

Let's say you grew up wanting to be a laboratory scientist. It's what you've always felt you were meant to do: wear goggles and peer into test tubes all day and maybe someday even discover the cure for cancer and win the Nobel Prize.

But whenever you mentioned this dream to your parents,

who play the violin (mom) and the bassoon (dad) for the local symphony, they looked skeptical and confused. This was hardly encouraging. And now you've just graduated from college with a major in music theory, which feels about as far away from a science lab as you could get, and you're blaming *them* for not having given you the right guidance.

If I tell you that the act of blaming, in itself, will hold you back, can you stop doing it?

For some, just knowing how destructive it is will be enough.

But for most, it won't be that easy.

So let's take it one step at a time.

The first thing to consider is that blaming is a way of saying, "Things should have been perfect." In other words, "I should have been actively encouraged by my parents to be a scientist."

But think of it from their perspective. For things to have been perfect for *them,* you would have been something else— like a violinist or a bassoonist, maybe. Or maybe you would have pursued another profession related to the arts. Anything but being a scientist, which they know nothing about.

Or which they just haven't had enough time to get used to.

See the problem? You view your future occupation one way, but your parents' perspectives are different. Which just means that all of you are human and have three different minds, all of which are moving along different paths.

*"But we're talking about me!"* you might say. *"My life!"*

Exactly!

And, ideally, they would have supported you. But for the sake of your peace of mind, there's a jump you (and we all) need to make, from acting primarily out of our childhood selves to acting out of our adult selves. The more we manage to make the jump, the more we can distinguish our aspirations from our parents'. Is this a simple task? No, I assure you. I've known 30-year-olds, 50-year-olds, and even 70-year-olds who forget to act out of their adult selves a lot of the time.

But here you are. In your twenties. If you can make some headway toward not blaming other people for what makes you unhappy, you'll save yourself from wasting a lot of precious time and energy.

So how do you do it?

By easing away, as much as possible, from the assumption that your parents should have been perfect. By understanding that your mother and father are probably "flawed" in some way—like you are, like everyone is. Perhaps you know that already.

Here's the thing: It's their right to be imperfect. It isn't anyone's right to hurt or mislead someone else, but people do the best they can—even when it comes out badly. And when it turns out in a way that disappoints you or drives you crazy, sometimes the best thing you can do for yourself is to say, "Well, now the ball is in my court."

Letting your parents (or whoever else may have let you down) off the hook—reminding yourself that they have their opinions and you have yours, and that's *fine,* and accepting that they may not have done things quite right, but you'll survive— launches you into your adult power. And this power goes a very long way toward improving how you feel about yourself and enabling you to draw good people and experiences to yourself.

The past is over. It's too late for anyone to have done anything differently.

Believe me. Most people have something to regret and something to overcome. Perhaps you do, too.

Keith Richards is a rich rock star, so maybe it's easy for him to smile at the past, but I still like to quote what he once said about blame. In the early days, the Rolling Stones were ripped off by everyone: promoters, record companies, concert directors, you name it.

Later, when referring to a former manager, Keith Richards said, "Am I angry? No. It was just the price of an education."

Well put.

I love that story, so I guess the only remaining questions are:

*But what about when you aren't a rock star?*

*What about when things aren't in the past?*

*What about when they're still going on?*

Big questions.

Read on.

# ANGER

Resentment is like taking poison and
waiting for the other person to die.

—MALACHY McCOURT

IT'S IMPORTANT TO DIFFERENTIATE BETWEEN getting angry
and being an angry person.

The first is a part of life. Like laughter, joy, or excitement,
anger can be a natural reaction to the world around you.

But then there's the second kind of anger: habitual anger.
It's the difference between being angry and being an angry
person.

Being an angry person is a problem.

Why does habitual anger often seem to develop after college?

Well, you're experiencing one of the biggest transitions
you'll ever go through, and transitions are emotional times.

But it's important not to let anger become a pattern.

Have you ever seen a deeply disturbed guy talking to himself on a busy city street? He thinks he's actually having a conversation with the person he's angry at, perhaps getting even in
his mind, but he's really alone. That's a good representation of
the problem with habitual anger. It's just a one-man show, or a

one-woman show. It's much like the problem with blame: We're giving the person who made the mistake *still more power* over us—the power to fix whatever went wrong—when what we *really* need is just to fix it ourselves.

*"Easy for you to say, Ken. But my mother (or father, or girlfriend, or boyfriend) is driving me crazy!"*

I understand. But this points us to a general question: When you get angry, can you deal with it, or does it stay with you? Do you hold on to it, or can you let it go?

❦

Imagine that you're living at home and you spill some orange juice. Your mother says, "You can't do anything right," and this makes you furious.

Whoa! Now the stakes are high.

If you deal with your anger in an effective way, you'll be free. You'll be primed and ready for whatever you really want to do. But if you deal with it in an ineffective way, well, you'll be carrying that emotional baggage with you for the rest of the day, and probably the day after that. So, the task is to deal with it in a good way.

Where do you begin?

It's helpful to start by understanding that anger's a secondary emotion. That means it's a reaction to something else, to an underlying hurt or fear that you might not actually recognize as the cause of your anger.

So this is where the real battle starts: finding your anger's actual cause and then dealing with it.

"*But Ken*," you protest (you're now shouting), "*my mother (or father, or girlfriend, or boyfriend) is driving me* crazy!"

I understand. But ask yourself: *What might be my underlying hurt or fear?*

First consider *fear*. Let's say that, living at home, you haven't found a job yet, you're down on yourself, you're yearning for your eventual independence, and you're feeling a passionate desire to create your first opportunity in the outside world. In other words, you're in a 24/7 struggle to stay on top of things and maintain a good outlook.

Pop quiz: In such a scenario, what would be the last thing in the world you'd want to hear?

"You can't do anything right!"

Yikes.

Let's face it. You know you *can* do things right and you're trying really hard, but in this example, the right thing hasn't come through yet. Enter the gremlins.

"*My opportunity will never come through for me. I'll be stuck here forever.*"

Not to mention "the big dog" gremlin who can sneak in despite ourselves: "*Maybe she's right.*"

Don't worry. She isn't, but it's hard to defend your outward actions when you're struggling with such inner fears. Or gremlins, as the case may be.

"*Fine, but did you hear what she said? How am I supposed to get anywhere in life if my own parents don't believe in me?*"

Of course, sometimes these comments sting. But how do you keep things moving?

Well, first, you'll probably clean up the orange juice. And

then maybe you'll get in the car and go for a drive and try to clear your head.

So, now tell me: *Can* you do anything right? Are you taking positive steps to make your life better?

If you can honestly answer yes to that question, then your task is merely to stay with the process, to keep doing what you're doing.

*"All right,"* you say. *"I'll keep thinking of positive steps I can take to make things happen in my life, to prove that I can do things right, and I'll follow through."*

Good.

*"But, ummm, Ken?"*

Yes?

*"Did you hear what she said? She said I can't do anything right. Am I supposed to just let that go?"*

I promise, we'll get there!

But let's stay with the hurt for a moment longer. Why would she say such a thing? Why would anyone say such a thing? After all, let's face it—it's not just your mother. Life comes with its own built-in frictions. This will eventually come up, in one form or another, with other people, too.

Why is it coming up now? Well, it can be for any number of reasons.

Maybe it's as simple as this: She's tired of having to clean things, and she's the type who has to do it before you even get the chance, which frustrates everyone involved.

Or maybe she's scared for you. Say that spilling orange juice implies to her that you're helpless in some way. A crazy idea, to be sure—everyone spills something now and then.

Or maybe that's what her mother (or father) used to say to her over small mistakes. These types of patterns tend to repeat themselves from one generation to the next. If she's critical by nature, someone was probably critical of her. But you can break this pattern. Instead of trying to hurt her back, or trying to get her to admit she was wrong or unkind, focus your energy instead on telling yourself that her criticism wasn't valid and doesn't apply to you.

Some more maybes: Maybe she has problems in her own life, and these make it hard for her to support you.

Or maybe she just cleaned the kitchen counter.

Or maybe . . . well, we could go on all day. Let's just say that we can't always be supported in the way we'd like.

Here's the thing: Focusing on another person's failure to support you in all the ways you'd like her to is sort of like saying that without that constant support, you're hopeless.

Ahem. You need to find a way to move on.

So do you respond in kind? I'm sure you've expressed anger with your parents before. Has it worked? It never worked very well for me when I was in my teens and twenties. It just made me feel, and seem, more like a child.

๑๖

Let's take a few examples of how your parents might provoke feelings of anger that can slide you into that category we mentioned earlier: "angry person."

*"They have expectations that pressure me."*

*"They criticize me."*

*"They're in my face."*

*"They don't leave me alone."*

*"They're trying to control me with money."*

With any of these, maybe you can talk to them and work it out. Some parents are going to be reasonable and open to coming to a mutual understanding.

But if not, maybe you'll need to find someone else to vent to, or go to an empty place and yell, or, as I'll discuss later, burn off some of this bad energy at the gym.

To take the solution further, the more responsibility you take for yourself, the better off you'll be.

For example, maybe your mom thinks she can criticize or control you if you're living in her house.

Is she right?

To an extent. If you're living in someone else's house, even your own parents' house after you've returned from college, you're not 100 percent on your own turf anymore, even if it's "your house," too.

But if the criticism and control go beyond this—if you're feeling like you can't do *anything* right, from not spilling anything to wearing the right shoes to sending out your résumé to enough of the right people—then the criticism is probably excessive. While respecting that your parents are people, too, with their own aspirations and the right to live happily and comfortably in their own home, take the necessary steps to stake out your own independence and, until you *are* independent, keep the peace as much as you can.

How do you do that when you're also under terrible pressure to find a job?

Or when you don't live at home but you still feel huge pressure from your parents to do something they want you to do, and right away?

The trick is to try to see the situation in a bigger way, as we're going to discuss in the next chapter.

∘✤∘

Before we move on, a few more psychological points about anger:

> Anger wastes the vital energy you need right now to accomplish your goals.

> When you blame or get angry with another person and it becomes habitual, the truth is that you're really angry at yourself, too. I don't mean you did anything wrong. I just mean that you're *in the process of being angry,* which is an uncomfortable state, and ultimately this uncomfortable state is not going to affect anyone else as much as it affects you. As I said at the beginning, it's a one-man or one-woman show.

> When you blame another person for something, or carry anger toward another person, you're going to feel guilty about it—even if you're right to be angry. That's just a law of nature. Why? Because there's a part of you, the part that wants to be free of the anger, that will be thinking, *Why am I letting this go on? Can't I stop this?*

Like I said, long-term anger, or resentment, is ultimately *your* problem. Not your parents', not anyone else's.

Yours.

Your anger is corrosive—to *you.* The emotion is a much

bigger problem for you than it could ever be for the person it's directed toward. So how do you stop feeling angry?

What I can say here and now is this: You cannot easily change other people.

But you *can* change how you react to them.

And what does this mean, in reality? I'm going to tell you.

Fasten your seat belts, because the next step isn't easy.

# CHAPTER 21

# FORGIVENESS

As long as you don't forgive, who and whatever it is
will occupy rent-free space in your mind.

—ISABELLE HOLLAND

WHEN I WAS IN MY teens and twenties, I felt a lot of anger
toward my parents.

Was it justified?

Some of it, yes. Some of it, no.

But, justified or not, it was a burden. It affected how I
viewed myself and how I perceived others. And it wasn't until
my late twenties that I was truly able to let it go.

You might well be thinking, *It took* that *long!*

But in fact, many people have burdensome relationships
with their parents all their lives—and often in ways of which
they're totally unaware.

It wasn't until I was in my midthirties that I began to understand why forgiveness is a central tenet of many life philosophies
and religions. Up until then, if someone wronged me, I tended to
lose my trust in the relationship and turn my back on it once and
for all.

Or, if I *was* actually able to express something like forgiveness, it was pretty much just a way to demonstrate to everyone

involved what a great guy I was. "Okay," I would say. "I forgive you."

But what I was really thinking was *You owe me one*.

And I maintained an inner scorecard of every relevant offense because I hadn't yet learned what a pointless waste of time and energy it is to keep an inner scorecard.

Later, I came to understand forgiveness differently.

Forgiveness is not about assigning guilt. And it shouldn't be about letting someone off the hook, even if that's a great added benefit.

I believe the true motivation to forgive is actually a selfish one. Forgiving other people lets *you* off the hook. It's the only way to move beyond the past.

To let it go.

"The best way out is always through," Helen Keller said.

And often the only way *through* is by forgiving.

Maybe you don't like the word *forgive*. Maybe it sounds too sappy.

Then how about this: How about *out-adulting* the person who's driving you crazy. In other words, being the bigger adult.

Why did I tell you to fasten your seat belt? Because I know this isn't easy. Or it may sound easy now—maybe you're curled up on the sofa with a Coke, and no one is pestering you, so you're feeling pretty good about everything—but it won't always seem so easy. Entire ancient religions are founded upon the concept of taking "the high road," precisely because it doesn't come naturally to us. The very phrase has become a cliché; people are always saying it, but it takes a lot of skill to pull it off.

∞

How does it work, in practice?

Let's say your dad is harassing you for not knowing what career you want to pursue. First, you'll try to reason with him. Explain to him that figuring it out is a process, and that to try to make some headway you are doing the following:

1. Researching career opportunities online

2. Seeking mentors and speaking to (name some people) for advice

3. Sending your résumé out to (insert places) and following up

And tell him, calmly, that if nothing comes of this strategy soon, you plan to try some new tactics. You certainly aren't just wasting time.

But what if he still looks down on you? What if he criticizes you?

Your assignment: Put on your running shoes, go out and run a few miles, yell at the top of your lungs if necessary, and then, with all that pent-up anger out of your system, keep thinking about what you're going to do, careerwise.

But also try as hard as you can to avoid criticizing *him* for criticizing *you*. Otherwise it'll turn into one big criticism party, and no one will get anywhere.

You need to forgive him, in your mind. (Or out-adult him, if you prefer.)

ⱥ

Another example: Maybe your mother has a habit of saying, "Why don't you call me when you're staying out late? I don't care if you stayed out all night at school. You're in my house now."

How do you respond? Well, you may consider talking it out with her, but if you've already had *that* conversation 10 times, you may not want to do it an 11th. So instead, you go for a long walk, or see a movie, or spend the weekend at a friend's. And then, once you've enjoyed some time away, think about how neither you nor your mom is exactly the person you want each other to be, and that's okay. Ideally for her, you would call at midnight every night to report your whereabouts. Ideally for you, she'd trust that you can take care of yourself. But because this is an imperfect world, you'll understand and tolerate her imperfection—and you'll agree to call at a certain time, even if it seems to you completely unreasonable.

Why? Because you're in her house, but only for the short term, and you have bigger challenges ahead and can't get stuck in the small stuff. And yes—this is small stuff. If you're being treated like a child, the best way to respond is *as an adult*. In other words, let it slide and make the phone calls.

Maybe you're thinking, *Okay. I'll be the adult if my mother (or father, or whoever it is) returns the favor. If I'm willing to make the calls, she should be willing to leave me alone. She knows I'm an adult, so problem solved.* But it doesn't usually work that way. Your mother may not want to meet you halfway. Or she may not be able to. There's an economy to forgiveness: It saves you the frustration and time of waiting for something that might never happen. Instead, out-adult her, and let yourself feel good about it.

Next example: Your father says, "You disappoint me."

Yeow!

Your assignment: Tell him you're going camping for the weekend—if you're the camping type. Or tell him you'll be back to continue the conversation in an hour, and until then, take a walk, work out, or go to that free meditation center (if you can find one). And while you lift those weights or chant the universal Om, understand that people won't always approve of you in life, but that you can still feel compassion for their lack of understanding. (After all, others are motivated by their own hopes, wishes, dreams, and fears; it's not always about *you* as much as you may think.) At the same time, you can stay on your path toward independence. After the workout or meditation session, stop at your best friend's house, vent, observe how your friend understands and supports you, take this as a sign that other people in your life will do the same, and then go home and tell your father how much you like his new haircut, his paint job, or scrambled eggs.

What's the philosophy here? Am I hoping you'll turn into a person who just gives in? A pushover?

No. Especially if the situation is much more grave than disagreements with your parents about curfews, job prospects, or even religion. The idea is that you save your energy for more important battles. Again, ideally, a parent will meet you halfway, but it doesn't always happen.

I once counseled a man whose foster father had beaten him years earlier. Now he was grown, and he dreamed of going back to the foster father's house, breaking in, and assaulting him.

What he didn't see was that by being caught up in this fantasy, he was still letting his foster father "win"—and his foster father hadn't thrown a punch his way in years. Why relive an old fight, especially one so devastating?

Our biggest pitfall is this: In adopting negative or even destructive behaviors, our parents (or guardians) teach us by example. Many people who were hit as children tend to grow up to become abusers themselves. But when Joe grows up and hits his children, he doesn't think to himself, *I'm doing this because Dad did it to me and I'm copying him.* He probably thinks, if he thinks about it at all, *This is how you behave in relationships. This is how you communicate and get what you want.* It's strange to think that we copy behavior we hate, but we tend to speak the languages with which we're familiar.

So the best "revenge" the man with the foster father could achieve—his most promising path toward liberation—would be to get out of this cycle and become something else, something other than a copy of his foster father, something other than a chip off the old block. In other words, to *not* be the guy who wants to resort to physical violence.

It's hard to do.

But I promise you that, no matter what the conflict, if you can let it go and move on—and for some people, in some very bad situations, this can take time—you will be much happier.

☙

The bottom line is this: Parents are big in our lives. "Should I deal with them or not?" is never really the question, because parents aren't like light switches. You can't just shut them off. And for a lot of people—like my friend at the lake (see chapter 15)—"refusing to deal" with a parent often results in exactly the

opposite thing happening: dealing with that parent all the time
in your mind. And if you're dealing with *any* upsetting person
or thing (even just in your mind), you're wasting precious time
and energy that could be spent helping you get on with a happier, more productive and enriching life.

Now that you're an adult, you want to look at your parents
at eye level, rather than gaze up at them. The ideal scenario is
the one in which, even if they drive you crazy, you love each
other and are a part of each other's lives, and this is most easily
achieved if everyone treats everyone else as the adults they are.

But if the history between you makes a relationship truly
impossible, if you've tried to make amends and no matter how
many times you out-adult a parent things don't improve, don't
beat yourself up about it: It's not your fault. You did everything
you could. The ball is in someone else's court now, and it may
never return to yours. Don't waste time waiting for it.

But in either case, always try to bear these two sentences in
mind:

*I am my own person.*

*No one can live my life but me.*

# PART 4

## PERSPECTIVE

CHAPTER 22

# STAYING UP

Worry is a form of fear, and all forms of fear produce fatigue.

—BERTRAND RUSSELL

LIFE IS WHAT YOU MAKE of it. We've all heard that.

Now consider this:

What you make of it depends on how you see it.

In other words, *perspective is everything.*

Do you know who Steve Ross is? He negotiated Time, Inc.'s merger with Warner Brothers. The result was—you guessed it—the megacompany Time Warner. As a major player in a movie studio and media conglomerate, he was friends with a veritable who's who of Hollywood's rich and famous.

And do you know what Steve Ross's first job after college was?

Selling women's bathing suits.

It gets even better.

After he got married, his father-in-law, who owned a funeral home, made him the director.

And after that he worked for a limousine business.

Years later, when asked about working at the funeral home, he said, "You service grieving clients at an emotional time in their lives. You learn about their needs and feelings. . . . There's no difference between that and the entertainment world. Both are people businesses in which the key is the ability to empathize."

But what if he'd stopped at square two—as a funeral director? Of course, he was lucky to have a family business to join. Not everyone has that opportunity. And undoubtedly there are people who enjoy owning or working at funeral homes. But I think it's safe to say that Steve Ross had other goals in mind for himself—and he achieved them by *staying up*. By "staying up," I don't mean staying awake, but staying focused, positive, and energized. In Ross's case, he managed to keep believing that things wouldn't remain the same but would instead improve over time.

That's the challenge for all of us. Imagine that you're the one who wants to be in the movie business and you find yourself working in . . . a funeral home. Not literally, of course. For you it might be in an entry-level job in an office somewhere, and you feel totally uninspired. What then? Can you keep going? Can you remind yourself that entry level doesn't last forever? Can you find a way to keep the negative voices at bay and make the experience into something good?

The bottom line: Life's going to deal you situations that fall short of what you want. It happens to all of us. Each time, you'll have just two options.

1. Lose hope.

2. Think about the situation creatively.

Successful people are not magically lucky at every turn. They don't land in the right job or with the best partner on the first try. They're just people who learn to use bad situations as springboards to better ones.

Someone once asked tennis star Martina Navratilova how long you have to practice to become a champion. "If you ask that question," she replied, "you'll never be one." To be a champion of your own life, you have to stay with it longer than you ever imagined, and stay motivated for the prize—whatever prize it is that you're after.

It's a fantasy to imagine that things will always just work out in life. Sometimes they do, but more often than not, we're tested. That's how it's supposed to be. And right now, post-college, you're probably feeling tested.

Big time.

Of course, if you're naturally optimistic and tend to see the bright side of things, you're at an advantage. But if you're not, there are skills you can acquire for *staying up*.

## WHY GYM CLASS WAS IMPORTANT

Sometimes we make deals with life, such as "I'll feel good about myself when the world gives me a reason to. Like when I get a better job. Make more money. Am in a serious relationship."

And yes, those things can make us feel good about ourselves.

But tell me, how do we get into a relationship? Often, when we feel good about ourselves, we attract the right person without even trying.

Oops!

And how do you get a job? You give other people a positive sense of who you are.

And how do you transmit that good vibe to other people? Exactly. You feel good about yourself first and project that to the world.

See the problem? If you wait for the good thing to happen, you'll continue feeling down. And if you continue feeling down, *it's less likely that the good thing will happen.* Which means you get caught in a cycle of low self-esteem.

So the trick is to feel good about yourself *before* the world gives you a reason to.

Where do you begin?

Simple.

Get up. Get out. *Work out.*

You may already realize how important exercise is; maybe it's a big part of your life. But if not, now's the time. Try to make exercise a regular part of this transitional period.

You'll look better.

You'll feel better.

You'll feel less stuck.

Less paralyzed.

Less worried.

Less *bad.*

So do whatever you like—weight lifting, walking, running, Pilates, cycling, swimming, ballet, basketball, yoga—anything that gets your blood pumping, your lungs working harder, and your muscles stretched out. Do whatever works for you.

❦

Here's another great thing about exercise: It makes you better at dealing with shock.

*"Huh?"*

I'll explain. Say you're walking down the street and a car honks its horn right next to you. What happens? Your heart jumps. You take a sharp breath, and temporarily you breathe a little more shallowly than you did before the honk. That's what happens when we're shocked: We disconnect from our bodies momentarily and breathe less deeply.

And in this disconnected state, we don't think as clearly or creatively as we do when we're relaxed. And you need a clear head to deal with the aftermath of any sort of shock or stress— whether it's something as unthreatening as a car horn or as potentially life-changing as a job interview.

When I'm in a Bikram yoga room and it's 102°F and I feel as though the world is ending and my head is swirling, I start breathing shallowly, and my feelings go from bad to worse.

Then it dawns on me, each time, that deep breathing is part of the practice and the way to pull through.

Later, when I'm back on the street, if I experience one of those little shocks, like the car horn, I find myself consciously taking a deep breath *just then,* when I need to, and the disruption barely registers.

Okay. The idea is not to train for the small stuff like a car horn, but to prepare for life's bigger shocks.

So if you're feeling bad about . . .

  1. Not having a job

  2. Not having a boyfriend or girlfriend

  3. Being broke and in debt

. . . then you, too, will probably start panicking and breathing shallowly. And in that state, you'll be a lot less able to come up with good solutions.

People who are relaxed breathe deeply.

And a calm state hooks you into your intuition, which is your inner guidance.

And exercise can also alleviate anger.

In general, it will help you feel better.

When we exercise, our brains produce endorphins, hormonelike substances that function as natural painkillers. The release of these transmitters often produces feelings of euphoria and a higher state of calm and general well-being. Also, the natural adrenaline rush that you get during a good workout conditions your body to control excess adrenaline caused by high-stress situations at home or work.

Show yourself that you're neither "stuck" nor "paralyzed" by pulling yourself out of that bed or chair and dragging yourself down to the gym.

Or the yoga studio.

Or the park.

Or a meditation class. Like exercise, meditation—and prayer, for those who pray—is a great way to calm down and relax. (If you've ever considered developing a spiritual life, now is a good time.)

⁂

During this period, you want to feel good about yourself. Maintaining your physical health will do wonders for your mental health.

CHAPTER 23

REFRAMING, OR
LETTING IT GO

Do not worry about your difficulties in mathematics. I can
assure you mine are still greater.

—ALBERT EINSTEIN

COLUMBUS DISCOVERED AMERICA. WAS HE a success or a
failure?

He was a failure if you take this into account: He was looking for India!

So it all depends on how he would have framed it.

If the frame was "Did I find India?" he failed.

If the frame was "Did I find America?" he succeeded.

∞

When I was in my twenties, a friend promised me a job in his big
firm. He was supposed to call me about it the following week,
but time went on and I didn't hear from him. I was pretty upset,
as you can imagine.

I thought, *It's hard enough when any potential employer
doesn't return a phone call, but a friend? That's an even bigger
insult.* And over the next 2 weeks, I revved myself into a really
bad state, focusing on that logic alone.

After another week of not hearing from him and driving myself crazy, I knew I had to do something. I couldn't focus on anything else because this little nonevent was hogging all my attention. I told myself that I just *couldn't* be upset anymore, and I decided to come up with a few "beliefs" that would help me let it go.

"To have a friend," I reminded myself, "be a friend." Oldest quote in the book.

So the first thing I decided was this:

He doesn't owe me anything.

It would have been nice if he had called, yes, but if I were really his friend, I'd let him off the hook. After all, don't we make those allowances for friends? Sometimes they forget to call, and we don't rake them over the coals for it.

Next, I decided this:

He thought I could help him in his business, but he's obviously changed his mind and just hasn't yet figured out how to tell me. As his friend, I'm not going to hold him to an informal commitment.

And finally I decided:

Maybe some aspect of his business has changed, and working for his company wouldn't even be a good thing for me. So maybe he's doing me a favor.

Having decided these things (i.e., having changed my frame), I was able to calm down and let it go. It also felt good to feel close to my friend again, even if he was a jerk.

Then guess what happened?

It was a public company and . . . I checked the stock.

Which had crashed.

I know what you're thinking. *Uh, Ken—why didn't you just check the stock in the first place?* Knowing that my friend's business wasn't doing well would have spared me weeks of anxiety and anger, right?

Yes. But only if I'd thought of it earlier—which, in my worked-up state, I wasn't able to do. I was just too upset to think straight.

And I was waiting for my friend to give me a reason to let go. But instead, I came up with *my own reasons* to let go . . . and then quickly discovered the real reason for his silence.

That's often how it works.

We often say to the world, "Give me a reason to stop worrying, and I'll stop worrying." But usually it's up to us to make the first move. We have to find a way to stop worrying, and *then* the world shows us something new.

When we find a way to be calm, the world opens up.

Likewise, if you're obsessed with an ex-boyfriend or an ex-girlfriend, but you're able to tell yourself something that allows you to let it go, life will usually reward you. You'll tend to glean new information that enables you to view the big picture from a healthier perspective.

I don't mean that if you cheated on someone, or just generally acted like a creep and someone's angry with you for it, it's okay to pretend you did nothing wrong. What I mean is this: If you can wish the person well in your mind and truly manage to separate yourself from the obsessed state, you'll probably learn something new.

What if you're waiting to hear back from a prospective employer and feeling that *everything* depends on the specific outcome of this pending event?

When you're looking for a job, waiting to hear back is big.

And what about not hearing back at all?

Listen. There are a lot of résumés floating around out there. You won't always hear back after you send yours in.

*"But maybe they didn't get it,"* or *"My mom says I should follow up,"* or *"My mom says she should follow up."*

Whoa! Let's start with that last one.

*Do not* allow your parents to contact prospective employers on your behalf! This is not about them; it's about you. All the people I know who make hiring decisions say the same thing: Employers do not want to hire children who need their parents to do things for them. (And by the way, this goes for everything after you get a job, as well—negotiating your salary or benefits, or reacting to your performance review, in the beginning or down the line. By all means, consult your parents for advice on what to do if you want to, but when it comes to dealing with your employer, do it yourself.)

Moving on.

You applied for a job and haven't heard anything. Should you follow up?

First of all, if you followed the application instructions, and if you sent your application by e-mail, and if you *can see the e-mail in your "Sent Items" box,* then it's very unlikely that your application hasn't been received.

If you sent it by snail mail, or if you're just dying to let the company know (again) how intensely interested you are in

working for them, then . . . sure. Follow up. But only very con-
cisely and unobtrusively, such as in an e-mail like this.

> Dear Ms. Evans:
>
> I applied for the job of marketing assistant last week
> and just wanted to emphasize my interest in the position
> and ensure your receipt of my application. If I may sup-
> ply you with any additional information that would aid
> my candidacy, I hope you'll let me know.
>
> Sincerely,
>
> Joseph Green

*"But my dad says I should call, and maybe it will segue into
a conversation."*

Unlikely, because the person you'd speak to is probably
either an administrative assistant or a receptionist. If you do
manage to get through to Ms. Evans, you will catch her off
guard and probably in the middle of doing something else,
which may lead her to think that you have insufficient respect
for her time.

What's more, well-meaning as it is, your dad's advice to follow up more aggressively could put you at risk of coming across
as too pushy and desperate. There is such a thing as trying too
hard—or trying the wrong way. You have to trust that once you
have presented your candidacy in a clear, honest, and polished
way, the right company will recognize you as a potentially valuable member of the team and offer you a job. You can only do
so much to try to convince someone to hire you without overdo-
ing it and putting the person off.

So, back to mental strategies.

You've applied for a job, and maybe also followed up, and now, if you're sitting around waiting for a reply as though it were a referendum on your life, you're going to get into a bad state. Maybe you're even beginning to think like this:

*If they don't want to hire me, will anyone?*

*If they don't want to hire me, will anyone want to date me?*

*If they don't want to hire me, does that mean I'm a loser, that I'll never get anywhere?*

Stop! This is madness!

If someone doesn't respond to your job application, you need to think of it this way:

1. *Maybe there is something I could do to improve my application materials.*

If you've done what you can to make your application materials the very best you feel they can be, and still an employer doesn't respond, tell yourself the following:

2. *This job isn't for me. I don't know why—maybe it's too advanced for me, or I'm too qualified, or they want someone older, or the person I'd be working for would make my life hell, and the person reading my résumé knows this—but it really doesn't matter. I don't need to know why. It just isn't for me.*

And *then* tell yourself this:

3. *The job that is for me is still out there! And this person who's not calling me right now is doing me a favor by allowing me to find it.*

And then do something else. Research some other job and career possibilities. Or, if you've already exhausted that angle for today, go for a run. Watch a movie. Invite some friends over for dinner.

In other words: *Let it go.*

Do the same thing if you feel stuck, like you don't know where to begin. This is another bad state, and it will do a number on your confidence. The remedy? Again: reframing. Try to learn to transform troubling situations into brighter-seeming ones so they don't zap your energy and motivation.

Say you still need a job, and what you're saying to yourself is *I need to get rich.*

How productive is that statement? What are you gonna do? Rob a bank? Play the lottery? Or maybe you'd go to work in a field that doesn't interest you because someone said you'd get "rich" there.

More likely you'd sit on the sofa, turn on the TV, watch people make money on an inane reality show, and feel bad about yourself.

The goal is to change "I need to get rich" into a better operating statement.

*"I want to make money."*

Better. But let's try a different one: *"I want to find productive work."*

How does that sound? Even better, right?

But will it get you off the couch or deposit a windfall into your checking account? No. And how exactly do you "find productive work"? Do you look in the closet? Under the bed? It's still sort of a nonstarter.

So how can we reframe it?

How about *"I want to figure out what interests me."*

I like this one. Let's break it down further.

*"I'll write a list of what I like doing."*

There. See? You've changed it to the extent that you can begin actually *doing* something.

Make out the list.

And when you come back to it, perhaps the next day, you can use it to formulate the next step you'll take, such as relating *what you like doing* to the skill sets those activities use and, in turn, to possible fields that make use of those skill sets.

Is that hard to do? If so, then you can first make a list of *whom to talk to* who might be able to help you connect those activities you like doing to their corresponding skill sets and to possible careers. Then, the next time, you can set out to schedule meetings with those people on your "whom to talk to" list.

⊙

Maybe the quicksand is this: *"I need to get married."*

I know, maybe this is not the first thing a lot of you are going to worry about right out of college—but then again, maybe it is.

If that's the case, let me summarize a key point from the Relationships section of this book: If you're desperate to get married, you probably won't attract the right partner.

So let's reframe this one to be *"I'd like to be in a serious relationship."*

This probably widens the field of prospects to a whole bunch of people who don't want to get married next week but who'd still like a meaningful connection.

But still, "serious"? Sounds scary, like it's not going to involve any fun at all.

Reframe again: *"I'd like to be in a relationship."*

Getting warmer, yes?

But this relationship, where do you find it?

You might check out a Web site geared toward matching people up. Or we can reframe this yet again: *"I want to meet people.*

*"So I should think of ways to meet people."*

And then you can make a list and the next day (or a few days later, or when you're feeling less pressure) begin to act on the points you've written out, which are the steps you'll take to meet new people.

&#8471;

The key to remember is this: When we're trying to set off in new directions, we sometimes present ourselves with overwhelming alternatives—too big to act upon—and those alternatives increase our feelings of hopelessness.

The trick is to transform the big ideas into workable steps. After all, as I'm sure you've heard, all great journeys begin with a single step.

CHAPTER 24

# FAITH IN YOURSELF

With the exercise of self-trust, new powers shall appear.

—RALPH WALDO EMERSON

FAITH IN YOURSELF IS LIKE oxygen, or water.

In other words, you need it.

Why?

Because even though we often perceive things as fixed in time, they aren't: They're always changing. And so are we. That means there's only so much about ourselves that we can know for certain in advance.

And *that* means that you have two options for proceeding.

1. Assume that you will deal poorly with every challenge life presents you.

2. Trust yourself to deal with challenges as best you can—and believe that this will be good enough. In fact, in a lot of cases, it will be *better* than enough.

Let's say you're a castaway on a desert island. You're surviving on very little food, and then, suddenly, a woman appears and gives you a seed.

You look at it.

She asks you what it is.

"I don't know," you say.

"Tell me what it is right now!" she says.

"Hey!" you say. "Hold on! I don't know what it is, and I need some time to figure it out!"

Then you could plant the seed and wait to see what comes up. No problem there.

But what if, instead of leaving you alone to get on with it, this woman said something crazy like "If you don't tell me what it is right now, then I can't let you have it."

Or even "If you don't know what it is, then it doesn't exist."

How could you possibly reply?

A. "There are many good forms of therapy available for you when we return to the mainland."

B. "Thank you, I've already eaten. Get off my island!"

In other words, her questions are clearly out of line. But how are they any different from what you put yourself through when you try to know exactly what your life is going to be like before it has happened? Or from thinking that if you don't know how life is going to be—what career you'll have, where you'll live, whom you'll be with, and so on—then you can't possibly be making progress?

I'm not saying that it isn't important to come up with a working plan for your career, some sort of temporary guidelines to pursue and follow. You do need to get started somehow, because the things you want in life are most certainly not going to just drop into your lap.

But your guidelines should not be too narrowly defined.

They should be flexible and open to change as *you* change. As you discover new things about yourself and about what makes you feel happy and free.

We don't discover these things all at once.

We plant seeds and see what happens. And then we adjust our decisions and movements accordingly.

◦∕◦

Here's another example of faith:

Think of a rosebush surrounded by fertilizer.

Think of the beautiful flower, the rose.

Now think about what feeds it: manure.

See? The beauty grows out of what's *not* beautiful.

It isn't really any different from knowing, in the throes of a breakup or a miserable job or even the death of someone you love, that something redemptive or even beautiful will come out of it.

We often have ideas about what would need to happen for our lives to work out "perfectly." But we've talked about perfection: It doesn't exist. It's a mirage. Expecting things to be perfect is like expecting the rose to grow without the fertilizer.

Instead, we need to trust that experiences, even "imperfect" experiences, are often to our advantage. We gain things we'll need down the road: perhaps a skill, a coping strategy, an awareness, or an understanding. In other words, the world sends us experiences that, when we work through them, eventually aid us in our progress. I know that's hard to accept. It sounds like I'm saying that the world is benevolent or paying attention to you personally. With all that happens, including wars, natural disasters, and random evil acts, it can be pretty hard to believe that the universe is playing any kind of constructive role in our lives.

But this isn't about the world being good or bad. We all experience darkness along the way. Faith in yourself assumes this: Darkness is part of everyone's journey.

Faith also assumes that the darkness eventually gives way to light.

The jazz pianist Herbie Hancock used to tell a story about when he was playing in a band with Miles Davis. During one number, Hancock accidentally played a chord that was off-key. He cringed and leaned away from the piano. But when Davis heard the chord, he took it in, and then ran with it: He played a few notes on his trumpet that somehow made Hancock's clunker not only fit right in, but even sound *good*.

Similarly, life sends us surprises, and we have to trust that, whatever comes our way, we'll have an opportunity to deal with them. We don't need every little thing to work out perfectly. We just need them to *work out*.

It's sort of like being a secret agent: We're told to go to a pick-up spot in 3 weeks' time to pick up an envelope with further instructions. Until then, we can't possibly know what the instructions will be. So we have to trust that when we do get them, we'll be able to deal with them successfully.

Even if the instructions, or whatever it is around the next corner, seem problematic, we still need to complete our mission.

Problems exist. They're *supposed* to exist. Problems mean you're *alive*. Once you solve the problem that's driving you crazy *right now*, another is bound to present itself. Remember: Life gives us hoops to jump through. The trick is not to wish them away, or to try to slink around them, but to take them one at a time and do our best.

Problems are the stuff of science, comedy, and art. Your challenges are as personally yours as your fingerprints are. When you deal with them as effectively as you can, little by little you add to your personal power, joy, and happiness.

Right now, all you have to do is take the *next* step, while trusting yourself and keeping your eyes open. The rest will take care of itself.

As you travel forward on your path, in the best way you can, in accordance with your best judgment at the time, the path will take you places. And you can trust that the places it will take you are related to where you'll eventually want to be. And that when you need to change lanes, accelerate through a sharp turn, ask for directions, or simply adjust your route, you'll know.

So go ahead.

Do it.

# ACKNOWLEDGMENTS

I'd like to thank Bette, Lisa, and Julie Will for their wisdom and vision; Liza Lerner for inspiring me to begin; Dianne Dubler and John Bigelow Taylor for their talent, friendship, and a wonderful shoot on the High Line; artists Claudia Alvarez and Terry Rosenberg for perspective and relief; Billy Shapiro, on call in LA, for helping me untangle a few knots; and, with love, my parents.

# INDEX

Underscored page references indicate boxed text.